REAR GUNNER PATHFINDERS

By the same author
I WILL REMEMBER AND OTHER POEMS

REAR GUNNER PATHFINDER

Ron Smith DFM

A Goodall paperback
from
Crécy Publishing Limited

A Goodall paperback

published by

Crécy Publishing Limited
Southside, Manchester Airport,
Wilmslow, Cheshire. SK9 4LL

Printed in Great Britain by
The Guernsey Press Co. Ltd., Guernsey, Channel Islands

The hills are shadows, and they flow

From form to form, and nothing stands;

They melt like mist, the solid lands,

Like clouds they shape themselves and go

But in my spirit will I dwell,

And dream my dream, and hold it true;

For tho' my lips may breathe adieu,

I cannot think the thing farewell.

In Memoriam

(Tennyson)

For my sister Doris
who always gave everything

For Heather
For her infinite patience in
preparing the manuscript

...and for that someone
who will always understand

Contents

Foreword

by Group Captain Hamish Mahaddie DSO DFC AFC & BAR.

(Acting Squadron Commander 7 (Pathfinder) Squadron, Station Commander, RAF Warboys, and Group Training Inspector responsible for the selection, recruitment and training of the Pathfinder Force).

I do Ron Smith no favours as a stand-in for Air Vice Marshal Don Bennett – sadly no longer with us – in attempting this Foreword. Able Over Charlie, as his Pathfinders dubbed him (but never to his face) would have found a sharper pen and keener words to emphasise the differences between each member of a Pathfinder crew but which, when merged into a single entity, produced outstanding rather than average crews.

We all felt stark terror from time to time and in different ways and our rear gunner had an outstanding skipper if judged only by the way he never transmitted his fears to the crew.

A Pathfinder crew had to learn that each crew member should be supportive of the rest of the crew. I devoured 'Rear Gunner Pathfinder' in a single sitting and relived the chill of 'Christ, not Berlin again'. I froze at the repetitive sight of aircraft going down in a second a black ball with a crimson centre and what the crews sometimes thought were 'scarecrows' (which never existed and in reality were aircraft). I shuddered at the near misses, related by our air gunner.

Nuremberg. We have all searched deeply into our souls about this operation that should never have taken place but Ron Smith will get no better answer to his 'Why, oh why?' than I can give after some years of research into that sad sortie. Perhaps the turmoil of mind can take some consolation from D.C.T., our Pathfinder chief, who strongly opposed the long, straight route to the target but received no support at all from the rest of the Command save from Roddy Carr of 4 Group.

I commend 'Rear Gunner Pathfinders' to all students of war and would-be historians and I trust that you, like me, having enjoyed and shared the full spectrum of emotions related by the author will find that our rear gunner is also by the way something of a philosopher in the making.

CHAPTER ONE

'Ten Minutes to the Enemy Coast'

Today would be a journey without return and, as the ancient tram droned noisily towards the centre of Sheffield, I moved uneasily on the hard seat. I was a little over eighteen and had left my job as a trainee dispenser with a multiple chemist. It was June 1940. Two weeks' previously I had volunteered for the RAF but my ambition to become a member of aircrew had been brushed aside by a busy recruiting officer. 'Enter as a ground gunner,' he had ordered flatly. Now I was on my way to Blackpool and basic training.

A few short weeks later, having been sworn in, sworn at, inoculated, kitted out, marched – it seemed incessantly – up and down the sunlit promenade, and having fired five rounds on the range from a vintage rifle, my basic training was complete. Along with sixty-odd other youngsters, I marched (in reasonably good order) to entrain for Perth, Scotland. Our duties – airfield defence.

Two years later, despite protests and repeated applications for air crew training, I was still there, and had been reluctantly tempted into a new formation – the RAF Regiment.

Apart from the frustration, I had enjoyed the intensive training. I had taken every opportunity to join various courses in gunnery: the Lewis and the Vickers machine-guns held no mysteries for me, and aircraft recognition had become second nature: I had fired the French 75 on the artillery range and won promotion. But always the return to our backwater in Scotland had made me realise how slim were any hopes of re mustering to aircrew.

Great was the excitement, then, when we were moved to Detling in Kent. Although the task was still airfield defence, there was at last a chance of seeing some action on this famous fighter station. Billeted amidst the orchards that surrounded the airfield perimeter, our unit settled in happily, although the daily helpings of plums and custard, with a liberal inclusion of wasps, soon began to pall.

Excursions to the local village dances were a welcome diversion, and it was at one of these occasions that I was fortunate enough to meet Anne, an attractive Wren who was stationed at nearby Chatham. I learned that her father was a senior staff officer in the War Office and, when making plans to obtain a leave together to visit her home, I suffered some disquiet at the thought of meeting this awesome individual and of what his reaction might be to the association of his daughter with a lowly corporal.

That confrontation, however, was not to be: one month after our arrival in Kent I was delighted to receive orders to report to the Air Crew Receiving Centre in London. A selection board awaited me, plus a stringent medical. If I failed I would be returned to my unit. The very idea of failure after the long years of waiting appalled me, and I could hardly sleep.

My comrades of such long standing did not help with their 'See you soon Smithy, have a good week-end in London.' After reporting my arrival at the Receiving Centre in the vicinity of St John's Wood, I was intrigued to find the place filled with fellows in civilian clothes, all more or less of my own age. As I took a seat and looked around, the atmosphere, with rows of chairs and their occupants lounging about in various degrees of boredom, reminded me of a hospital waiting hall.

As the only serving airman there, I began to feel more confident of getting through. It had not occurred to me that anyone would be there direct from civvy street. Although I thought my past service should give me advantage, apprehension still prevailed when I remembered what was at stake.

The waiting seemed interminable. At last, we were directed to an ante-room, test papers were handed out and a time limit set for each subject. Handing my completed papers to the officer presiding, I left the room more concerned than ever. The maths paper, particularly, had been more difficult than I had envisaged.

The next few days were taken up by a thorough medical examination. As I had been confident of my fitness, I was shattered to find that I had failed the colour vision test. It was only after a further test that I was passed 'defective safe' and, subject to the final interview with the Selection Board, might be considered for training as an Air Gunner.

And so it was to be. I was accepted by the Board, my previous Gunner Training having swayed the decision.

I entered upon my new career enthusiastically, although the subject matter of hydraulics, pyrotechnics, control of the Fraser Nash turret with its four Browning machine-guns and sighting, deflection, etc. was complex, my previous experience stood me in good stead and I had little difficulty in achieving the high standard demanded.

The weeks and months of hard work culminated in a final posting to Morpeth in Northumberland, where we were to receive practical experience of operating our turrets under flying conditions. There were further live practices with the Brownings until we could find and diagnose a stoppage blindfold.

My initial air-sickness subsided, although I still remember swallowing the vomit that rose in my throat during the fighter affiliation exercises.

As the Blackburn Botha was thrown about above the North Sea I had to pass instructions for evasive action to avoid the mock attacks of a determined Spitfire pilot. I endeavoured somewhat desperately to keep the attacker in my sights and allow the correct deflections. A combination of the nauseating smell of fuel-oil, dope and the sickly reminder of the turret's previous occupant, with the sight of the coastline far below rising to an impossible angle as the aircraft dived, was nearly my undoing. Thankfully I retreated from the turret and down the fuselage to allow the next gunner to take my place.

Towards the end of June 1943, we sat our final examinations. I was delighted to find I had passed with a good percentage to spare, and the great day arrived when we assembled on the parade ground to receive our long-awaited sergeants stripes and air gunners wings.

The notices of posting to operational training units appeared, and I couldn't believe my eyes when I read '1351882 SMITH R to OTU Doncaster', only a short distance from my home.

I was none too happy arriving at RAF Finningley on my own. Before this posting I had always been a member of a group – the old adage about safety in numbers takes on a special significance in the Services, because if you are uncertain of yourself you can always sit back and let someone else find out what is going on.

Collectively, there is a sort of joint learning which you can improve on for yourself once the introduction to the new environment has been overcome, while initially preserving your own anonymity. With these courageous contemplation's in mind, I approached the main gate of the largest RAF Station I had seen so far.

Operational Training Unit meant exactly that. We met and flew with the men with whom we would go on operations. Generally speaking we were allowed to make up our own crews. For the first few weeks we received advanced training in our own particular field. After our pilots had completed their conversion on to Wellingtons we would continue with crew training.

I was finally approached by a tall, quiet Canadian sergeant pilot Jack Cuthill from Richmond, British Columbia – later to become a S/Ldr with the DSO DFC who asked me if I would like to complete the team he had assembled. The navigator was Geoff Thornycroft, from Manchester-a cheerful individual to whom I took an immediate liking. The observer/bomb-aimer was Bob Trotter, from Durban and at first sight a little aloof but, as often is the case, a warm, kind individual when one really got to know him. The wireless operator, Ross Tobin (known to us as Toby) was an Australian from Melbourne, who, unlike many of his countrymen, was rather shy and introverted.

We were all rather aloof at our first meeting: after all, when you are going to put your life into the hands of complete strangers, you are entitled to be a little cautious. You want as far as possible to make the right decision, although at that early stage, you could not possibly be sure how any individual, including of course yourself, would stand up to the stresses of operational flying.

Now that the real training was to begin, it was up to the individual to ensure he carried out his designated task as efficiently as humanly possible – not only for his own satisfaction and preservation, but for the benefit of everyone in the crew.

We progressed to practices on the nearby bombing range, then on to cross-country flying, and eventually to long, night exercises. These activities gave all the crew valuable experience, and, although I was little more than a passenger for many of the exercises, I began to feel at home in my turret. The occasional air-to-sea gunnery practice became quite an event, but, in conjunction with the other members of the crew, I was settling in, and although we did not at first recognise it, we were gradually building a trust in each other, all centred on our skipper. He was completely relaxed and unshakeable.

Our training continued until we could undertake the most ambitious exercise with confidence and appreciable success. Finally, with five other crews, we were briefed for an operation over enemy-held territory, a diversionary sortie over France to attempt the bombing of a Divisional Headquarters at Forêt d'Hesdin. We recognised this as the real thing at last, and listened with mounting excitement to the briefing officers.

We took off in the dusk for the flight to Northern France, and I shall long remember the spark of fear as Geoff announced, 'Ten minutes to the enemy coast'. Suddenly, I saw a string of light flak ascending at some distance, and self-importantly yelled out the information at the top of my voice, only to be told to 'Shut up' by our imperturbable skipper.

We dropped our bombs and turned for home. I took my eyes from the glow far below, remembering the Gunnery Leader's warning that looking at the target was none of my business. I strained my eyes to search the surrounding darkness and rotated the turret from one side to the other, always with the uneasy feeling that when I was looking to one side something would creep up on the other. I ended up swivelling around continuously, much to the annoyance of the skipper, who could feel the effect on the controls. then, feeling rather aggrieved, I steadied up the rotation and concentrated on a systematic search in all quarters around the rear of our aircraft.

We returned without incident – feeling like true veterans. We ended our first operation not fully appreciating what was to come.

Our time at Finningley was at an end. We moved on to Faldingworth in Lincolnshire and our introduction to the mighty Lancaster, four engines and a mid-upper turret, necessitating two more crew members, a flight engineer and gunner.

We were introduced to Tony Briton, our engineer, who had been posted direct from St Athan in Wales, and was a bright engaging personality, soon to become the crew comedian. Nothing seemed to get him down and later his occasional impressions of Popeye the Sailor man over the intercom lightened many a hairy situation.

Dougie Aspinall from Doncaster, our new mid-upper gunner, appeared shy but soon settled down happily, and we considered ourselves fortunate to have acquired two such obvious assets. Our crew was now seven.

The skipper, aided by Tony, handled the conversion to the Lancaster in his typically efficient manner. There was, for me, little new to learn, as my turret was identical to the one I had left behind at Finningley.

A few weeks later we were posted to an operational squadron at RAF Wickenby, closer to Lincoln. We arrived in the October drizzle.

CHAPTER TWO

Operational

We entered the Sergeants' Mess that evening to a different atmosphere. Due to heavy losses in the last few weeks the Squadron was sadly depleted. The remaining occupants stood around in groups ignoring us completely; they seemed a world apart and 'looked' different. Some of the terms they were using, when snatches of conversation could be overheard, were unfamiliar, relating to their experiences over Germany. As we left the ante-room leading to the exit to find the small Nissen hut allocated to the crew, a definition of the complex fabric of their aloofness eluded me. Not a word passed between us as we followed the path towards our quarters and we all experienced a profound humility, as if we had intruded upon something sacred. These sobering thoughts were not lifted by the scene as we entered. The place had been left, no doubt inadvertently, exactly as it was the previous evening by the crew who had not returned from a raid over Berlin. Personal belongings were everywhere, sheets turned back on the beds, and at the side of the bed I had chosen, on a small locker, photographs of a pretty girl with a signature and sentiment to the absent previous occupant. We tidied up, placing all the items of personal value together in readiness for collection.

Becoming reasonably established in our new quarters, we discussed the events of the day, particularly our impressions of the manner of our introduction to the Squadron. The banter and gaiety of our normal behaviour was noticeably absent; even Tony, the crew comedian, lying on his bed pensively smoking a cigarette, was unusually subdued. Finally, he and I decided to take a walk before turning in. When we reached the perimeter track that ran around the airfield, I could see in the half light the black silhouettes of the Lancasters at their dispersals, brooding in their silenced grandeur. I shivered involuntarily as a cold wind stirred the scattering of leaves from the low trees at the side of the hangars. We retraced our footsteps to our quarters and I reconciled myself to sleep. Tony's final words echoed in my mind, 'I hope they don't have to collect our personal stuff for a while, Smithy'!

After breakfast, we were welcomed by the Flight Commander in his office below one of the hangars. A brisk cheerful type, his manner raised my spirits immensely, especially when he intimated that the heavy losses suffered by the Squadron were unusually high and way above the average. In his opinion this would level out and he proposed further cross country training for all the newcomers for the first week or so. We dispersed to our various sections, Dougie and I reporting to the gunnery leader, a Flight Lieutenant wearing a DFC ribbon under his air-gunner's wing. Flight Lieutenant Jackson after two tours of ops still flew operationally once a month, usually with the Flight Commander. Looking at his massive bulk made me wonder how he managed to squeeze into a gun turret. Along with the other gunners from the new intake to the Squadron, we crowded into his tiny office which led from the main section building. He came straight to the point, dismissing the pervading gloom that had settled over the Station. We listened to his detailed advice, a lot of which contradicted what we had been previously taught. As we filed into the Gunnery Section proper, my morale had improved considerably, though secretly I was relieved at the respite gained by the Flight Commander's promise of further training. As a matter of fact, we flew only two exercises, both to Scotland and back, but this enabled me to get some valuable practice firing at markers dropped by Bob off the coast.

Almost a week later we learned that Jack, our skipper, was to fly on his first operation without us, joining another Squadron crew as second pilot for experience. We assembled along with other watchers beside the runway to watch the Lancaster's take off in the late afternoon. With some disquiet at the thought that we might lose our skipper, I silently wished them Godspeed and a safe return as they roared down the runway. The following day, when we pestered him about the trip to the Ruhr, he made little of it as far as he was concerned, but he took pains to impress upon us the lessons he had learned, and sharply reminded us of our inadequacies.

Later that week we were down for operations. In answer to the tannoy, we left the mess to join the other crews in the Briefing Room. The blinds were drawn, with station police at the door, as our Wing Commander took the platform, and outlined the operations for that night. As the huge wall map was uncovered, showing the UK and most of Europe, with tapes tracing our route to the target, Geoff nudged me in the ribs to whisper, 'Not Berlin for Christ's sake, what a place to go for our first bloody "op"!' I agreed as I listened with mounting dismay to each Section Leader dealing with his aspect of the sortie and its concern to the individual crew members. After navigation, signals, bombing and gunnery briefings, came meteorological and, lastly intelligence, which gave warnings of the flak positions along our route. A final summing-up by the Wing Commander, in which he emphasised how essential it was to stay with the bomber stream, also to bomb the markers left by the Pathfinders as accurately as possible, ended our first briefing.

As some last minute instructions and adjustments to flight plans were being given to the others, Dougie and I walked slowly along to our quarters. We discussed our zigzagged route across Europe to the target and back – the usual practice to confuse the fighter defences – and which on this occasion turned off abruptly at the last minute, on the approach to Magdeburg, before the final run-up to Berlin. It seemed a perilously long way and I arranged a system with Dougie that would ensure a constant surveillance by one of us of most sectors around the aircraft. I was fully aware that the onus for our defence against rear attacking night fighters rested principally with me. An appreciation of the implications of our imminent ordeal across Germany only added to my determination to give as good an account of myself as possible. Later, in the locker room, as we dressed carefully before being taken out to our aircraft, there was some leg-pulling amongst the crews, and Tony raised a laugh by parading up and down in his long underwear, doing his inevitable Popeye impressions.

Our Lancaster, M for Mother, was positioned almost at the other side of the airfield. High-spirited remarks and cat-calls followed the crews as they were dropped off at their dispersals, until we reached our own aircraft where the ground crew waited. The skipper signed the Flight Sergeant's sheet, acknowledging that he accepted the aircraft as serviceable (earlier that day we had flown an air test which had proved it). We stood around, chatting and smoking while we waited for the time to arrive to start the engines. Although there was always a possibility the op would be scrubbed, even at this late hour I did not allow the thought to linger for long, as I was mentally prepared and impatient to get on with it, and the waiting became irksome. Chewing chocolate from my flying rations, which Geoff had collected and shared out, I checked again that my escape kit was safely zipped up in the pocket of my flying suit. These kits contained European currency, compasses, maps and condensed Horlicks tablets-invaluable if one had to bale out over the other side.

The time approached to start engines. As the ground crew brought up the trolley accumulators we donned our parachute harness, Bob laying his spread-eagled on the concrete, joking at me that this was how I should look before the night was over. The silence was shattered as the engines started intermittently around the airfield. Climbing the ladder into the aircraft, I made my way down the narrowing fuselage towards the bulkhead door that divided the aircraft from the rear turret, noting the ammunition belts in their metal channels, running aft from the boxes like miniature railway tracks down to the servo feed and up to the guns. I secured my parachute to the side of the fuselage with the elastic hooks provided and dropped down into the turret. Bob Trotter patted me on the shoulder, giving the thumbs-up sign, which I returned as he closed the bulkhead door behind me. Reaching round, I pulled the sliding doors of the turret together, latching them securely. After plugging in my intercom, I settled down as comfortably as possible, sweating in the bulk of my flying suit and Mae West inflatable lifejacket.

The aircraft shuddered, coming alive as the engines were started one by one. With all four engines running, they were revved-up as Jack and Tony did their checks. At last, with chocks pulled away, the Lanc ambled slowly out of dispersal to join the queue of aircraft moving along the perimeter to the runway. As our turn came to line up for take-off, I glimpsed the preceding Lanc roar past on its way, the exhausts belching flames until it disappeared, obscured by the control van near the runway edge. Acknowledging the skipper's query, 'OK Smithy?' with an affirmative, as he braked to a halt, I checked the turret was locked dead astern. A brief pause and again his quiet voice, asking for full power, still holding the straining aircraft momentarily, until on release, we moved off, WAAFs and airmen waving frantically as we gathered speed. The tail came up, lifting the turret high off the ground, and I watched the tarmac fast slipping away, raising my hand in salute, as I always did, in the superstitious belief that, if I forgot the gesture, we should not return. A sinking feeling as the wheels left the runway, the tail section descending slightly and the Lanc hesitant with the overload of bombs and fuel. As we picked up speed, I felt the dull thud as Tony selected the undercarriage up, and soon heard the skipper ordering flaps up also. As we gained height, I looked back at the airfield, glad that we were on our way. The tension eased and I was more relaxed than I had been since briefing earlier in the day.

With the superb Rolls-Royce Merlins straining to lift us to operational height, I heard Geoff give the skipper the first course to steer. As the ground disappeared in the murk, I could see scores of aircraft climbing slowly upwards, silhouetted against the light still in the sky above. Fastening my oxygen mask, I adjusted the flow, feeling a slight light-headedness as my brain adjusted to the pure oxygen. The freezing air began to penetrate through the bulk of my layers of clothing, in which I had been sweating earlier. I was grateful for the warm tingle around my body as the electrically heated undersuit began to warm up.

The skipper's voice again crackled over the intercom, checking each crew position, receiving the familiar 'OK skipper' as we roared on, speeding towards the open sea and the next change of course. A glance behind and to each side showed the massive fins and rudder towering up and looking solid and reassuring, trembling slightly as the aircraft shuddered through an air pocket. Feeling rather warm, I reduced the heating and, receiving the skipper's permission, fired a short burst from the Brownings, all four of which responded instantly. The sound of the guns, so shattering on the ground, was muted by the roar of the engines. I adjusted the reflector sight until the glow of the circle lost its glare. Rotating the turret smoothly, I checked with Dougie that he was watching the starboard quarter behind me. On his confirmation, I stood up, searching the dark void behind and below.

An alteration of course, for our run-in over the enemy coast, allowed me a glimpse ahead. Anti-aircraft fire, streaming up like coloured fireworks, heralded the reception waiting for us, then lost to view as the aircraft straightened upon the new heading. 'Keep your eyes open!' Jack's voice warned as, diving slightly, we roared across the coast. A terrific crack, as flak burst almost alongside, left me stunned for a brief moment – my first experience of close enemy fire. Not a sound came over the intercom until a few long seconds later, and then the skipper asked if we were all OK. Our mid-upper gunner from his vantage point on top of the fuselage replied: 'That was bloody near, I'm sure we were hit.' Everything seemed to be in order, however, as we penetrated deeper into enemy territory.

The weather had deteriorated – dense cloud without any sign of a break.

I constantly rotated the turret, ever searching for that darker patch that might show up against the blackness around to indicate an enemy fighter. It was a relief when the aircraft entered cloud for a short time, its protecting folds hiding us from prying eyes. As we came clear, I had a paralysing sensation that we were not alone. Looking around frantically, I could not see anything until I glanced upward through the perspex top of the turret and there, almost on top of us, was the massive outline of another Lancaster completely overshadowing us. As I stared hypnotised, tiny rivulets of moisture formed moving patterns on the curve of the perspex as the slipstream compressed the droplets picked up in the cloud. I could see flames from the exhausts streaming back under the colossus above, as with a dry throat I switched on my microphone and croaked a warning to the skipper. His reaction was instantaneous: we dived steeply, lifting me almost to a standing position although I was held by my flying boots firmly entrenched below the gun mountings. The huge shadow above appeared to shoot upwards and away.

As we resumed our course, two of the crew demanded to know what the hell I had seen, as my instructions to the skipper had been: 'Diving turn to port, go! ' – the standard procedure when attacked from that direction. Before I could reply, the skipper called for silence, leaving Geoff cursing at the loss of his navigational equipment, which had shot all over the place during our violent manoeuvre. The phrases I used in those horrifying seconds had been spontaneous, although not technically correct. The skipper's handling of the aircraft reassured me as I resumed my vigil, wondering uneasily why Dougie had not seen the Lancaster a few feet above him.

Our last turning point came up as we left Brunswick to port. As the cloud thinned I could see the flak coming up heavily with searchlights fingering the night sky. Someone had blundered over the city off track and was suffering for it. As Geoff passed the course to steer, I felt our aircraft turn slightly to port for the final run to the target. I saw more flak over Magdeburg where a tiny flame flickered, then streamed back as an aircraft fell out of the sky. A few seconds elapsed before a burst of light suffused the cloud below as the unknown hit the ground.

An exclamation from Bob, way up in the nose of the aircraft, that he could see flares ahead, indicated the target was near. Our skipper's quiet voice confirmed that he also could see the target, with a further reminder to Dougie and me to keep our eyes open. I continued staring out into space, constantly searching from one side to the other. Flares bursting slightly to the right, as I sat with my back pressing against the turret doors, made me re-double my efforts. I called the mid-upper, demanding to know if he could see anything, and waited impatiently for a reply. Then suddenly we were over the Big City and I was petrified at the ghastly panorama all around. After the long hours of searching the night sky from the coast to be suddenly propelled into the brilliant hell over Berlin produced a freezing of the mind. As I gazed in awe at the multiple unfolding horror I felt exposed and vulnerable.

Flak sliced up through the broken illuminated clouds, ascending gracefully, to scream past the turret. A Lancaster slid across at right angles with a single-engined fighter just behind it, as if attached by an invisible thread. The city far below was bubbling and boiling, splashes of fire opening out as the blockbusters pierced the terrible brew. Forcing myself to look above, as had been drilled into me so often, I was appalled to see a Halifax with gaping bomb doors. As I stared the bombs came tumbling out to arrow down just to one side of us.

Bob called for bomb doors open, as he could see the red phosphorus target indicators, released by the Pathfinders, dripping down. His 'left, left, r-i-g-h-t, steady,' instructions to the skipper, as he lined up the bomb-sight on the pulsating mass, were given as if he were detached from the terror below. At last, the upward lift as the heavy load was released; then, with full power and the nose down, we raced towards the blessed darkness ahead. High above I saw two fighters dip their wings to streak down as they attacked a Lancaster behind us, breaking off as the bomber burst into flames. It remained on even keel, flying on, as if ignoring its mortal wounds. Tiny figures fell away, one after the other, to fall through the white canopy of cloud into the inferno far below, while the Lancaster wearily drifted down, suddenly to accelerate and then disappear for ever.

We reached the protecting darkness – the skipper demanding a course for the first leg home, Geoff hesitant and unsure, at last passing it to him. I looked back as we banked away, and saw the target glowing like a boxing ring in the centre of a vast auditorium. My morale had recovered somewhat, since we were heading for home, but I was ashamed of the secret knowledge that I had left the aircraft defenceless over Berlin. If a fighter had attacked at that time, I was convinced that I would have been too shocked to reply. The rest of the crew, apart from Bob and our resourceful skipper, had maintained a thoughtful silence, broken now as Jack checked each station over the intercom to receive affirmatives all round.

We droned on and on, with an occasional flicker of flak in the distance. It soon became obvious from Geoff's discussions with the skipper and Bob that we were lost. Geoff climbed up into the astrodome, a perspex blister at the head of the fuselage, to try for a fix with his sextant. After some time, while we waited anxiously, he worked out a course. The skipper swung the aircraft on to the corrected heading and we resumed our journey across the endless sea of cloud. Without warning, all hell broke loose: the flak seemed to be an impenetrable barrier. The skipper changed height constantly, throwing the Lancaster around in a desperate attempt to avoid the bursting shells. The starboard outer engine failed, and Jack yelled at Tony to feather it, altering the propeller pitch to minimise drag. A violent explosion immediately above me sent the aircraft plunging down, a huge hole appearing in the starboard fin. The turret would not answer to the controls and I used the manual handle to bring it dead astern.

I prepared myself for what seemed to be inevitable, and my thoughts centred on my inaccessible parachute. The flak increased to a crescendo and I could hear the shrapnel hitting the fuselage. A long stream of petrol reached out behind us from the port wing. I yelled out to the skipper but could not catch the reply as multiple explosions bracketed the aircraft. The petrol continued to stream out behind us, until it slackened and then stopped altogether as the self-sealing compound worked in the tank.

I began to think of my family and what the reaction would be if I did not return. After a lifetime we left the hell behind, losing height as the port inner engine lost power, to backfire and splutter, picking up again and again, until we crossed the enemy coast at last. A final parting burst of anti-aircraft fire followed us out as we limped on over the sea.

If, as we assumed later, Geoff had put us on the wrong track (owing to an understandable navigation error on his first real 'op') over the heavily defended Ruhr, the German gunners must have been mortified at our escape. As we pressed on the skipper warned us we might have to ditch if the complaining engine gave up. With Bob's assistance, Geoff managed to obtain a fix on the Gee Box, now in range of the transmitters sighted on the coast. The problem remaining was of insufficient petrol, and Tony constantly reported to the skipper as our supply dwindled. Anxiously as time sped by Jack asked for an ETA (estimated time of arrival) at the coast. After calculation Geoff's estimate was that it was touch and go as to whether we could make our landfall. We were now down to four thousand feet, and through the intermittent cloud I could just catch a glimpse of the cold North Sea below. Removing my oxygen mask, I rubbed my face where the mask had chafed the skin, feeling its sting around my mouth. I fumbled for the packet of cigarettes, and lit one gratefully, drawing the smoke deep into my lungs. A cry from Bob that the coast was just ahead put new life into my limbs. I craned my neck to see ahead but could not get round far enough. Geoff suggested a landing at Woodbridge, just inland from the Suffolk coast, where a special runway had been built for just such an emergency as ours, extra long and wide, with crossed searchlights marking its position. Receiving the frequency from Tobin, our wireless operator, Jack called for permission to land. As we had no resources to fly around the circuit, it was a welcome voice from Woodbridge control which came back almost at once with landing instructions, warning the skipper to watch out for other aircraft in the vicinity. Tony selected the undercarriage down, but was unable to obtain an indication that it had locked into position, while the ailing port inner engine failed completely after back-firing noisily.

The skipper went straight in and suddenly we were over the expanse of the runway. As Jack held off I watched the tarmac coming up and racing by behind me. Bracing myself as the aircraft hit hard, I felt the undercarriage collapsing. Showers of sparks were reaching back, with the screech of rending metal. Helplessly, I watched as the tail section swung in an arc, the Lanc spinning broadside on to the runway, and finally coming to a shuddering halt.

Reaching behind me, I wrenched open the turret doors, pushed hard on the bulkhead door, and fell into the fuselage, flat on my back, while the intercom connection flex, becoming bar-taut and painfully twisting my neck, pulled my helmet off. Scrambling to my feet, I stumbled along the fuselage to jump after Geoff on to the hard ground, and to stagger after him to get away as quickly as possible.

As we grouped together, looking back at our gallant aircraft, a Jeep came racing up to screech to a stop. Out jumped a Wing Commander to ask if anyone was hurt, and it was only then that Bob mentioned his miraculous escape, when a chunk of razor-sharp shrapnel had pierced the fuselage, to touch him across the thigh and smash through the other side of the aircraft. There was a neat gash across his flying suit where the metal had penetrated, leaving a shallow cut in his flesh. Our bomb aimer refused at first to leave in the ambulance that had arrived, and we walked over to the crumpled Lanc. Riddled with holes, the fin almost severed in half, she looked a write-off. Talking excitedly, we recounted our versions of our dreadful trip, until eventually Bob went off to sick bay, and we were driven to a small hut for a welcome mug of hot tea laced with rum.

Bob rejoined us after having his wound dressed and we were informed that there were no facilities for us to stay. Purely laid down for emergencies, Woodbridge consisted only of the extensive runway with a few outbuildings, so accommodation had been found in the small nearby town of the same name. With the assurances that our kit, and especially Geoff's navigation bag containing restricted and secret information, would be taken care of, we were driven into town to a small hotel.

There was a private function still on at the hotel, and when word went around of our presence, the welcome was unbelievable. Plied with drinks after a sumptuous meal, we joined the dancing, dressed in battle dress and flying boots and temporarily forgetting our exhaustion.

In the early hours I awoke, desperate to find a toilet. Staggering out of my room attired only in long woollen underwear, unshaven and with hair awry, my ears still ringing from the roar of the engines, I found myself in a long corridor. In my bemused state, I firmly believed I was in an RAF billet somewhere, and after trying the handle of a bathroom door demanded the occupant to 'pull his finger out and let me in'. At the sound of the catch being released I stepped forward, to come face to face with a pretty girl, who took one look at the apparition before her and promptly screamed. Retreating hastily I stumbled back to my room until the hubbub had died down; then, past caring, I opened the window on to a small balcony, hoping there was no-one passing underneath.

The following morning, at breakfast, still suffering from the effects of our op and too much alcohol, I was embarrassed at the look I received from my ill-met female, who entered the breakfast room with her father and mother. Derogatory remarks from my crew mates added further to my discomfiture.

When we arrived back at the airfield our aircraft appeared more forlorn in the cold light of day. They had dragged her on to the grass alongside the runway and one could now see extensive flak damage. The port fin nearly severed, riddled with holes and a gaping rent near the main spar, right through the starboard wing. Just forward of the rear turret the damage was particularly disturbing, this, where I had heard an exceptionally loud explosion, I imagined, immediately beneath me at the time. When I reflected on the possibilities of what may have happened, if that shell had arrived a fraction of a second later, brought home to me how much the element of luck had played a major part in our survival.

Railway travel warrants were arranged for our return to Wickenby; as we left, the Wing Commander's parting words remained with me, 'Good luck you chaps, I'm proud of you.'

I instantly felt a bit of a cheat. Looking around at the other lads, I couldn't help but wonder what their reaction would have been, had they realised that my performance over Germany, and especially Berlin, weighed heavily on my conscience. Hidden from them, way back in the rear turret, I was judge and jury myself, the verdict, as far as I was concerned did not bear thinking about. Perhaps they also nursed secret fears. My own mind was dominated by the fact that if our recent terrifying experience was our first op. what the hell would the others be like?

A minimum of thirty trips to Germany before a rest period was granted seemed totally and utterly impossible and completely undermined my earlier determination to give a good account of myself. I was not to know this was a perfectly natural reaction and it would take some time before I could become remotely acclimatised to living with the constant fear of death.

The train journey back to Lincoln was spent discussing the events of the previous night, at first soberly, then inspired by Tony's satirical remarks, boisterously until, by the time we vacated the compartment at Lincoln, we were laughing and joking at each other's discomfiture and at our individual experiences and reactions during the ordeal of our first real op over Germany.

Interrogation followed at Wickenby and we re-told our story in the Mess, listening attentively as our comrades related theirs. Much later and very drunk, we staggered back to our billet. I for one, to sleep exhausted and oblivious to the doubts and fears of the past forty-eight hours.

Before lunch the next day I walked to the Mess with Tony. Finding a quiet corner in the ante-room I opened and read letters from my mother and Anne. Mother's concern was obvious, not having heard from me in the last few days. I hastily scribbled a reassuring note and posted it there and then. When I thought of her, alone in the house that had kept her so busy and happy, with the family all around her, I was immensely saddened and suddenly ashamed that recent events had erased the thought of her from my mind.

Anne's letter was predictably petulant, although she had some excuse. My letters to her had become more and more infrequent, even those I had sent were short and must have betrayed my irritation at her obvious concern with herself, although at this time, her selfishness had not completely extinguished my feelings towards her. Somewhat ungraciously, I began to pen my reply, only to be interrupted by Geoff gleefully informing me there were no ops that night and suggesting we join a game of poker before getting ready to go out on the town. We returned very late after a glorious fling in the pubs of Lincoln, whose inhabitants showed a kindly toleration towards the air crew invasion. The welcome we ourselves enjoyed lasted throughout the war for those who followed. Lincoln was being surrounded by mushroom airfields hastily built into the flat countryside.

In the Mess the following morning, Tony said we were down for ops that evening and an air test had been arranged in the aircraft we had been allocated. As Dougie, the mid-upper gunner, and I approached the Lanc at dispersal to check our respective guns I felt the hard knot forming in my stomach again. The cheerful face of the armourer, clambering out of the turret did little to dispel the feeling of foreboding. I did the check automatically confirming the armour's 'They're spot on Sarge'. Sitting in the tiny compartment, I re-lived the events of a few days earlier, not allowing myself to be reassured by the chatter of the crew, who had now taken their places for the air test. Bob's buoyant observation, 'It'll be a piece of cake tonight lads', sounded hollow and false. I remembered his white face and how tight-lipped he had been before our last trip to Berlin; I fervently hoped Geoff would not get lost again.

Driven back to flight later, I wondered at the skipper's relaxed confidence; saying very little and lacking any bravado, he seemed to exude the essence of reliability. Feeling somewhat reassured and immensely grateful for that we joined the others at briefing.

If familiarity breeds contempt, then I can only say that although my immediate surrounds – the turret, its controls, my view of the night sky, still faintly illuminated on a winter's evening at 18,000 feet, by a sun that had set some time before – were familiar, my feelings were far from contemptuous. It was far too early in my career, as far as operations were concerned, to accept with any equanimity the mind-numbing fact that again I was being accelerated backwards through a limitless void, towards the enemy coast and the hell over Western Europe.

One or two of the more experienced gunners had intimated, after anxious prompting, that although Frankfurt – our target for that night – could be dicey, it was a piece of cake compared with Berlin. Much as I wanted to believe this, some desultory bursts of flak, at some distance from our aircraft as we crossed the Dutch coast, led me nervously to report the occurrence to all concerned. The ensuing silence made it obvious that exclamations were totally unnecessary. Nothing untoward happened as we droned on, far above the invisible landscape, as the weather gradually worsened. I wondered about the inhabitants far below and what it was like to be ruled by the German invader.

Geoff, who seemed to be on top form with his navigation, called out the course for the next turning point. The Lancaster responded to the skipper's new heading, heeling over to starboard. Without warning, the blackness all around was brilliantly illuminated by a string of flares bursting almost alongside us, where seconds before we appeared to be completely isolated. With startling clarity, I could see several Lancasters all around, above and below us. Rotating the turret, I strained my eyes, striving to pick out any enemy fighters, and unable to believe that attack was anything but imminent. As darkness closed about us once more, I stood up in the turret, trying to see behind and below, endeavouring frantically to regain my ruined night vision. Resuming my seat, I hear a babble in my ears as all the crew tried to speak at once. 'Will you sons-of-bitches wrap up! ' came the skipper's Canadian drawl, bringing silence. His next instruction-'Smithy! Dougie! For Christ's sake keep your eyes open' – was hardly necessary, as mine were out on stalks already. For a moment I felt strangely comforted that other Lancs were around, and selfishly weighed the odds that they would attract the attacker and not us. I stood up in the turret again, vainly searching for a darker patch than the void around us that would indicate another aircraft, while our own weaved gently to put off any interested night fighter.

We were to contemplate later how a gun position underneath the fuselage, similar to that possessed by the Yanks, might be an advantage. German Me-110s were using upward-firing cannon, and sneaking up beneath the unwary bomber, to fire a burst straight into the petrol tanks in the wings. The Lanc, of course, carried a much heavier bomb load than the Fortresses, and I expect the designers knew what they were about. I don't think any of us would have swapped aircraft: affection for the Lancaster and its utter reliability was not in question.

All other thoughts were quickly driven from my mind as Bob reported flares being dropped over the target, nearly covered by cloud, thinning here and there to reveal the sparkle of countless incendiaries already doing their work, interspersed by eruptions, as the heavy bombs found their mark. Flak-bursts all around, another Lancaster appearing, almost alongside, with bomb doors open shedding its load. Again that bemused and bewildered mind of mine tried to grasp the meaning of it all. Bob's irritatingly calm voice, as he passed his instructions to the skipper. The Lanc skidding first left and right, my whole being willing Bob to drop the bloody bombs anywhere and let's get to hell out of it, in reality saying nothing, nothing to betray the myriad fears.

At last, bombs gone, the Lanc lifting free. The indescribable satisfaction, that we were not on the way in any more, but going home. The dog-leg, leaving the target to starboard, where I could see its glare out of the corner of my right eye, was almost completed, when another Lanc crossed behind us in a flash, so near that I yelled 'Look out', without having time to switch on my microphone. I followed up this useless reaction by informing the skipper (who grunted a reply) just as uselessly, for the offending bomber must by then have been miles away.

On and on, through the blackness, and as each few minutes passed, daring to hope that we may get back all right, not yet letting my mind dwell on our distant base and its welcome of interrogation and indescribably delicious mugs of hot tea, laced with rum. At last Geoff's voice, 'Coast coming up', and we were over, soon leaving the dark frontier, to the open sea and England. Still I rotated the turret, ever searching, never relaxing. Other aircraft, calling up the airfield for permission to land, even before they reached their circuits, hoping against hope that they would not be kept waiting. The WAAF controller's impersonal voice, giving instructions as to what height to circle base as she 'stacked up' the aircraft at 500 feet intervals, until their turn to land. Impatient voices on the intercom, ignoring RT procedure, demanding to know if the pilot before them had gone on a cross country, as it was taking him so much time to land. Jack's calm voice, 'Undercarriage down, full flap.' The runway unrolling in front of me, the drumming of the landing gear, taxying to dispersal. A last cough from the engines, climbing down the ladder on to the firm concrete, Dougie's observation 'That's another one done, Smithy.'

Crew bus to operations for interrogation, saying little unless asked. Volunteer WAAFs, trim and alert, handing out mugs of tea. Bacon and eggs in the mess, walking down to the billet, keeping to the narrow concrete, a last cigarette, climbing between the sheets. Sleep at last, the noise of the Merlins still invading the consciousness...

As I closed the door of our Nissen hut, one of several isolated from the main thoroughfare of the airfield, it was pretty obvious, weather wise, that Christmas 1943, due in a few days time, was going to be traditional.

Snow had fallen heavily all day, followed by a hard frost,

while grey clouds, relieved of their heavy burden, moved reluctantly aside, revealing a brilliant moon and its attendant stars, reflecting the white familiar landscape all around, stark, still, in its clinical cleanliness.

Looking forward to the evening's festivities, my footsteps dulled by the crisp snow, I made my way towards the airfield's main group of buildings and the WAAFs' party to which we had been invited. I was in no particular hurry, my mind debating the events of the past few weeks, and in a nostalgic mood, to which, I must confess, I had always been prone. I felt no antagonism towards the gods of chance who had brought me here, at this time, but thoughts of home and Christmases past which could never be the same again, combining with the recent loss of my father, brought tears involuntarily to my eyes. I brushed them away impatiently, vaguely and unjustly implying that the biting wind, which swept across the airfield, bore the responsibility.

As I approached the long, low building with its curved, corrugated roof, typical of the economy of war-time construction, dance music became clearly audible, the willing but amateurish efforts of the camp musicians authenticated by the friendly tones of a saxophone, and interspersed by the stomping of many feet. Inside I was almost immediately accosted by Dougie, his honest Yorkshire face flushed already, and his accustomed shyness lost with the help of a few pints of the local brew. He held a pint glass in one hand, his other arm around a diminutive WAAF. 'Where the hell have you been, Smithy?' he yelled, 'Geoff and Bob are at the bar, you're about eight pints behind.' As the evening wore on I found myself alongside a mixed group of WAAFs and airmen, trying to harmonise the latest Glenn Miller ballad. As a loud cheer greeted the final chorus, I caught a glimpse of the pretty, smiling face of a young WAAF wireless operator who had claimed my attention before when I had to visit the control tower after an air test. I remembered returning her amused glance as I had tripped over the matting as I entered; also the tall, well-modelled figure, almost stately as she walked ahead of me down the corridor, the general indefinable look of high breeding and the natural simplicity which nearly always accompanies it. A wealth of auburn hair completed the picture. At the time, with other things on my mind, I had made a mental note that this girl I must see again, and here she was, dancing in the arms of a Warrant Officer whom I vaguely remembered seeing in the Mess. His uniform carried no air crew insignia, so he must have been on the administrative staff; then I remembered an argument with him over the exchange of some flying boots at the equipment centre, and his reluctance to issue a new pair. He appeared much older than his partner, but there was no doubting his good looks.

I was conscious of an unreasonable jealousy, resenting the familiar and intimate way he was holding her. It was obvious that they knew each other well and were not just casual dancing partners. I mentioned my observations to Tobin, who appeared at my side in his dark blue Australian battledress. From my description he knew the girl immediately. 'You've no chance there, mate,' he volunteered, 'She's going out with that stores bloke, you know, the one you had the row with. Her name's Tina something or other.' At least I knew her name and sidled off down the room as the band leader called a break, searching the sea of faces anxiously, to try and catch a glimpse of her again. As I reached the buffet, I saw them hand in hand. Her face flushed from dancing, she looked unutterably lovely as I stared miserably across. The food I held remained untouched. 'If you don't want that, I'll have it,' Bob's cheerful voice at my elbow. I passed it to him. At that moment, I caught her eye and held her gaze unashamedly. Although there was no suspicion of a smile as she turned towards her partner, I was aware of an indefinable something that had passed between us. Before the dance was concluded, I noticed her looking across at our group on at least two occasions. I make no excuse for this narrative of my second encounter with Tina, for she was to have a profound influence on my life.

The following day, after more snow, the entire camp was paraded to draw shovels to help clear the runway. Despite the tomfoolery and high spirits, the job was completed as the early winter's night closed in on the featureless, flat landscape. Christmas Eve at last, yet none seemed to know what was going on. Ops were unthinkable, although the day was fine if bitterly cold.

In the crowded Mess, the usual opinions were being expressed, when unbelievably the news arrived that ops were 'on' that night and air tests were to be carried out forthwith. Profanity was in the air as we cleared the Mess. If the powers that be could have overheard and witnessed the bewilderment we were feeling, perhaps the decision to go would never have been made. One almost comes to expect that Christmas, of all holidays, is sacred everywhere, even on the other side. It was not the time off duty that mattered, but the improbability of a raid at such a time, when some sort of unofficial truce could be expected. Strategically, the basis may have been sound, but I remember a strange disquiet and a feeling of revulsion at the prospect, which was heightened later as we assembled at briefing to find take-off time at 00.15 hrs-no longer Christmas Eve.

When the target was uncovered, the timing of the raid was no longer the main concern. The target was Berlin, that most hated of all objectives, which again filled me with foreboding. With take-off so unusually late, we returned to the billet, each occupied with his own thoughts. I lay on my bed, my mind filled with turbulence, and wrote and left the usual letter to my family.

We had been promised a party to end all parties in the Mess the following day on our return ('if we return', I thought). The very idea of succumbing on Christmas Day seemed almost disgusting. As we chain-smoked the intervening hours away the general opinion was that we might take them by surprise, though the long route out denied much hope of this. I was grateful for my flying clothing as we boarded the crew bus to be taken out to dispersal. Snow ran across the tarmac in flurries and I wondered how takeoff would be. My feet shot from under me, hampered by my parachute and an armful of flying rations, much to the crew's amusement. Remarks such as, 'Look out for Father Christmas', 'It's no good hanging your stocking up tonight, Smithy', as we were dropped at our aircraft, cheered me enormously. We climbed aboard and I settled down as comfortably as possible, feeling that sense of relief now we were in the aircraft, and the waiting was over.

The four Merlins were soon running smoothly. I listened to the usual cockpit checks and we again joined the queue, taxying around the perimeter to the end of the runway, halfway around the airfield. As we received the 'green' and turned on to the runway proper, I saw that an unusually large crowd were assembled, even at the late hour, to cheer us off. I had the sudden notion that Tina might be there, and waved frantically back as, at the release of brakes, the Lanc slowly gathered speed. As most humans do in times of dire stress, I called upon God for courage.

The snow coming down heavily now, speeding past in a slanting blur, the Lancaster coming off, then sticking again, as the runway hurtled by. The full load of petrol for this trip held her down to the last minute, before she finally lifted over the fence at the runway's end and began to climb soggily above the white Lincolnshire countryside. I double-checked that my electrically-heated suit was working, as it seemed a long time before any warmth could be detected. Gradually, I felt the comforting tingle, and had to adjust the intake. My oxygen mask felt cold and uncomfortable when I fastened the mouthpiece, and I pulled at it irritably until it was settled more comfortably.

Eight and a half hours to go-equal to a full day's working time – breathing the life-giving oxygen, constantly searching the freezing void all around for any sign of other aircraft. The enemy coast at last, through patchy cloud, the glimpse of the white expanse below. Searchlights stabbed their exploring fingers over to starboard, as the German ground defences woke up to the fact that this was a major raid. Over seven hundred aircraft around, an invisible armada of destruction. Seven men in each aircraft huddled over their instruments, certain in their own minds that it would not be their turn to die tonight.

Flashes from below in quick succession. Avoiding action, the Lanc banking away, as predicted flak-bursts appeared in the space we had just vacated. I pushed a benzedrine tablet under my mask and tasted its bitterness – tablets that would keep your eyes firmly open when your body was exhausted, mind ever alert, but sometimes distant, unbelieving. Suddenly the great expanse of the target, as we crawled across the brilliant white cloth of cloud obscuring the city burning below. Aircraft all around, above and below. Few fighters tonight, but look out, never let up, bomb doors closed, now to get back. A yell from Dougie: 'I think there's a Halifax just below us.' The Lanc dropping like a stone as we bank hard to starboard in a diving turn, an Me-110 with twin aerials shooting past above us. With the square wing tips showing clearly, Dougie's error of recognition was understandable. He had only caught a glimpse as we were weaving slightly from side to side. A farewell burst of flak sliding up through the cloud in brilliant elongated strings and exploding all around us, then the blessed darkness, welcoming, all-enveloping, a respite, a respite from the mouth of hell.

Geoff passing the course home, the weather worsening, condensation dripping from the valve in my oxygen mask to freeze upon my face, the skin around, peeling away, sore and irritating. Then a sight that would haunt my dreams for years after, a sudden gush of flame streaming back from the wing of a Lancaster, almost alongside us though unseen until now; tiny figures dropping out, one, two, three, four and no more. The flames stretching back until the whole aircraft is engulfed, the night as day, and the tiny silhouette of the night fighter breaking away underneath, its grim task completed. Another minute figure dropping away as the remains of the bomber plunged down through the cloud and you wondered about the other two crew, locked in that flaming wreckage, to be spattered across the frozen land far below. The void closes in and we drone on, ever on, towards that distant Dutch coast and the gateway to living.

At last we are there, the weather now tossing our aircraft about like a leaf, over the invisible North Sea, through huge canyons of cloud that look solid enough to walk upon, finally breaking up into towering frozen columns we are leaving behind. Crossing the English coast at last, to see the outline clearly, the white breakers crusting the shore. The voice from below, instructions to land, undercarriage down, the giant wheels skidding over the snow-covered runway, along the black outlines left by the previous aircraft.

When we had reached dispersal, and the engines were finally at rest, I sat for a minute. I had now completed four ops, if the first one from Finningley could be included, and the prospect of doing another twenty-six before a rest period, again assailed my mind. If I had then been aware that this would be extended to sixty-five, I would have dismissed the very idea as totally impossible. And if I had known that the majority would be performed with Pathfinder Force, I would have denied the forecast of the future as tea-leaves in a cup.

But I am ahead of my story, for little did I know that I was becoming captive, even at that early stage of that unexplainable ambivalence of starting to live anew after each return yet, overcome by the imponderable enormity of it all, reluctant to vacate the turret.

In the interrogation room, the shuffling crowd of air crew, awaiting their turn to face the intelligence officers, crowded for mugs of tea. As I accepted mine, I suddenly became aware that Tina stood there at the far end of the room, looking at me thoughtfully. Her answering smile led me to ask her to the party that evening. Later I found out that she had volunteered her services that night and, I was pleased to hear, had been anxiously awaiting my return.

All the ingredients were there to make the party memorable, everyone determined to make up for the previous evening. If any thought was given to the two crews who had not returned, no one was showing it.

In the early hours, I walked Tina to her quarters, to hold her very close, knowing that although I was fond of Anne this was totally different. As I walked slowly back to the billet, the thought that I had much to lose unsettled my mind, and I became most uneasy-a feeling I thought I had discarded.

CHAPTER THREE

Berlin Again

It was midweek before the Squadron assembled in the briefing room for further operations, and the usual speculations as to the intended target were bandied about by the rows of anxious air crews. From what I could overhear, their predictions did not seriously include Berlin – it would be rare to visit a target so often.

Looking around, I marvelled at the outward composure displayed by those who had all but completed their tour of thirty operations. Having as yet had little opportunity to get to know them all personally, I was awed to hear that several were on second tours. We were called to attention, and in the silence that followed the wall map of Europe was slowly revealed.

A groan of disbelief from a hundred throats filled the room. I stared numbly at the route tape, reaching out and across to Berlin after all. The CO called for silence, then read out a personal message from the C-in-C Bomber Command, Air Marshal Sir Arthur Harris, emphasising (half apologetically, it seemed) that the Battle of Berlin was as vital to the conduct of the war as any yet undertaken.

The fact that he found such a direct and personal message necessary disturbed me, a tiny cog in the complex organisation of Bomber Command though I was. That he, who supervised a force that was expanding at such a furious rate, should send replacement inexperienced crews like ours to face an ordeal of such magnitude again so early in our operational careers, seemed to me akin to the actions of a First World War general. It was our third briefing for such a major target, out of a total of five ops to date.

We were already aware that losses were becoming increasingly unacceptable, and surely new crews should have received their initiation attacking less demanding targets? Experience in our profession was not just desirable but essential. The highly complex task of taking a modern aircraft at night to find a distant target, so fanatically defended, and to return safely, needed a very special kind of person – and an element of luck.

Later in Pathfinder Force, though never immune to fear, one became confident in one's fellow crew members when facing the most arduous and near-suicidal missions, with that inborn sense of unity, tinged with not a little arrogance and pride that provided the ingredients vital for survival: split-second reactions, almost faultless navigation, and a liaison between pilot and gunners resembling the uncanny.

My somewhat dazed dismay was rudely interrupted, as the crowded room filled with noisy conversation, and briefing came to an end. 'Come on, Smithy – move – pull your finger out', as the mid upper-gunner tried to push past, and the hubbub of voices became less animated, to quieten altogether at the exit, as if each man had become immersed in his own thoughts.

At dispersal, a light covering of snow outlined the tracks of the crew bus as it continued on its rounds, delivering each crew to their aircraft. Looking back across to the distant Control Tower, I longed to see the arc of Very lights indicating that ops were scrubbed.

A sense of foreboding, much more deep-seated and active than the usual pre-op nerves, was still predominant, unaffected even by the wisecracks of our engineer, Tony.

Under a threatening sky, as the daylight began to give way to the winter night, snow intermittently swept across the half-covered concrete, to eddy around the undercarriage of our waiting Lancaster.

Again the ritual of a reluctant last look around before climbing the ladder up into the cavernous fuselage, shuffling along on my backside, until I could drop down into the turret. As Bob closed the bulkhead door that sealed the turret off from the aircraft proper, his 'thumbs up' was little consolation. Once more to draw the curve of the sliding doors behind me, locking them securely and settle in for the long ordeal.

Our Lancaster ambled along the perimeter towards the distant runway. The snow came down obliquely now, cutting across my vision, and the Lancaster immediately behind, its four great propellers whipping up the snow into clouds of white smoke, was almost obscured by the powdered mist created by our slipstream. No last minute reprieve now, even in this weather.

We get green, a scream from the brakes as the skipper turns on to the runway. Once more the glimpse of waving figures to my right, lining the first hundred yards, and we are off, slowly, oh, so slowly, gathering precious speed, until hesitantly we leave the last of the runway, and I watch the boundary fence fade into the thickening gloom.

I wondered if Tina had been able to see my frantic gestures before take-off. Thoughts of the previous evening, dancing in Peterborough-I could see now the finely arched eyebrows, her glancing up in that shy way, filling me with tenderness.

The perfect circle below, airfield perimeter lights that signified home, gradually retreating as the straining engines take us up into cloud. Another last glimpse before obscurity, and we are enveloped totally. How I detested ascending through cloud, or alternatively descending through it for that matter, sitting there feeling supremely helpless.

Cloud over Europe, to enable us to hide from the ever-growing attention of enemy fighters? Yes. But climbing through the stuff, sat on top of a full bomb load, or descending to circle base on return, in the close proximity of other aircraft, made my blood run cold. A glimmer of light, the dirty cotton wool rushing past, and we are above an endless plateau of cloud, the perspex all around losing the opaque covering.

Last of the sun on the far horizon, the sky's darkening blue and another Lancaster appears, thrusting through from the morass below, the sensation of speed dispersing as we climb ever higher.

Heat and oxygen on, I listen numbly to the crew's chatter,

the reprimand from the skipper, Geoff's voice giving a change of course, and we bank away to port.

Over the sea I test the four Brownings, the thud-thud-thud as they react to slight pressure on the firing buttons filling me momentarily with satisfaction. Four lines of tracer reaching out astern produce momentary blindness (later most tracer rounds were taken out of the ammunition belts for this very reason), but how comforting this night though, to watch it curve away.

Now I can see aircraft all around, above and below, all fighting to reach operational height. Suddenly the flight engineer's voice, reporting that the starboard outer engine was overheating.

I take little notice, anticipating that it will settle down, until Tony speaks again more urgently this time, passing on his fears to the skipper.

Gradually a discussion arises, the whole crew taking part; suggestions that we abort the operation are being made. Our pilot demands silence. Did I detect, for the only time up to then and in our long future association, a vestige of uncertainty in his voice? Finally the decision to return was taken.

The journey back was made in a strained silence, as if we were all secretly ashamed.

Back at base, we faced the CO's disbelief, for to abort without very good reason was not taken lightly, and the skipper received instructions to report the following morning, after the offending engine had been inspected.

An uneasy drink in the Mess, and I called Tina. She was pleased at my early return, and could not quite understand my dejection.

I am sure we all felt that we had failed in some way, and were subdued and concerned for the future. What action would the CO take if the engine was found to be in working order – functioning enough to have enabled us to carry on?

Had our introduction to operations over Germany, severe as it had been, influenced a decision to return which should never have been made? Had we, as a crews taken our share of that influence by almost to a man declaring it was of little use to go on? Had we let down our pilot and friend, irrespective of the fact that the final responsibility for the decision was his? The news that forty-two aircraft failed to return set the seal on our mortification.

The skipper's feelings, after a stormy interview with the Wing Commander, who had queried his confidence in the crew, led him to vow to us all it would never happen again. Blaming himself did not help, but from that day a new purpose burned within us: we had much to live down, especially within our tight little circle.

That evening we drowned our sorrows. The following day, two days before New Year's Eve, we were down for ops. The target was, of course, Berlin. I sensed a quiet determination that night as, once again, we were outward bound for the enemy capital city. Hardly a word broke the silence on the intercom, except for the calm voice of our skipper checking that each of us was OK.

A flak ship off the enemy coast opened up. I saw the flash of his guns far below, the shells exploding above and to one side, then more flak as we headed inland and banked to the new course given by Geoff. Nearly complete cloud cover as I watched another Lancaster, silhouetted slightly below, edge slowly away.

'Don't be proud-stay with the crowd', proclaimed the posters in the flight section back at base, and there was a dire reminder of that warning when a flicker of flame became a flaming torch in an aircraft way off to starboard, and then another in the same vicinity. The invisible bomber stream round us afforded some protection from enemy fighters as long as we stayed with it, for the hundreds of bombers blanketed the enemy radar. Stray out of it, and you were easy meat for the marauding fighters, vectored on to your aircraft by the enemy controllers in their sections that ringed the coast of Europe, becoming ever more efficient and deadly in their unfailing determination to inflict increasing losses on our comparatively defenceless bombers.

Out of the corner of my eye, I'm sure I see a dark shape moving overhead from my upper right. The turret answers to the pressure applied to the controls, the hydraulics lifting the guns in unison. I am relieved to see the silhouette of another Lancaster pass slowly to be lost in the darkness.

Sweating slightly, I adjust the power flow to my electrically heated inner suit, comforted by the gentle weaving action maintained by the skipper, providing some defence against surprise attack by any unseen fighter.

At last a sight of the target, lighting up the surrounding darkness as we turn in for the bombing run. Suspended again over that pulsating hell, trying to resist the temptation to look down – to concentrate above and all around, but with my burning eyes being dragged back to peer below, as if by a magnet. The inevitable, coloured strings of balls of flak, floating up through the cloud in perfect symmetry, to explode with a crump as they flash by. The gritty noise, the heavy stuff making our aircraft shudder in protest, losing height and yawing to one side as we are bracketed viciously, the skipper fighting for control. Bob's voice as the bomb doors open giving precise instructions, 'steady – left, left – right – steady', and in my overwrought imagination, I picture the 'cookie', four thousand pounds of high explosive, nestling in the bomb bay surrounded by the thousand pounders, unprotected, vulnerable...

Bombs away but we still seem to hang suspended over the inferno, no sensation of speed – so slow. I search continually, full ninety degrees, thumbs on the firing buttons, rotating the turret right to left, left to right.

High up on the port quarter, three enemy fighters streak down to fasten on to a fleeing bomber. As the third one breaks away, the Lancaster maintains its course without offering evasive action suddenly to explode in a ball of fire, pieces of debris floating down, nothing recognisable as the proud, invincible machine with its seven man crew that was there a few seconds before.

The fighters dive away in the opposite direction, so emphasising their speed, and I tear my eyes away, searching, ever searching, until once again in darkness.

The target still visible over fifty miles away as we head for home, 'How long to the coast?' I ask Geoff. He exaggerates the distance, thinking (as he told me later) that Dougie and I might relax our vigilance if we knew the coast was imminent. He had no cause to fear for I had no intention of letting up until we were well out over the North Sea, beyond fighter range, and even then of keeping a wary eye all around me.

Nearing the Norfolk coast, I can at last remove my oxygen mask and light a forbidden cigarette. The confined space allows little opportunity to stretch aching limbs, but the mental relaxation gives a euphoria that brings me near to tears with the knowledge that I have survived again.

Down, taxying to dispersal in comparative silence, directed to a space almost at the perimeter end. I decide to walk back to Intelligence.

The freezing air welcome on my face, flushed with the relief of our return. Had I really travelled from this spot to Berlin and back? The enormity of it all overwhelms me. My fur-lined boots hurt my heels as I walk along, rubbing continuously, sore and irritating. Hearing the crackle of exhausts as another Lancaster touched down over to my left, I thought about the crew of the exploding bomber over the target.

During interrogation I had an opportunity for a few words with Tina, looking so neat and untouched by events, adding further to the contrasts of my existence. Ribald remarks from the crew, as I hurried after them to the Mess, each of us vying with the others to re-live our experiences all over again.

CHAPTER FOUR

On to Pathfinders

In the Gunnery Section the following day, Dougie hurried over towards me, his face flushed with excitement. 'We have seven days leave from today, Smithy,' he said, 'then we are posted to Upwood in Cambridgeshire for training to join 8 Group Pathfinder Force.' To say I was taken aback would be putting it mildly. The elation that filled me to hear the magic word 'leave', a respite for a whole week, was tempered by the astonishing news of our posting.

'How could we have been accepted for Pathfinder Force?' I queried. 'The skipper volunteered a few weeks ago, Smithy,' replied Dougie, enjoying the consternation on my face. 'He didn't let on, as he thought we wouldn't be accepted, especially after that balls-up the other night when we aborted.' 'They must be pushed for crews,' interjected another gunner smugly. 'They must be getting the chop right and left.'

Tina could not believe her ears. We had arranged a night out in Lincoln and she was far from consoled when I suggested that I left for home the following day, so that we could at least spend one evening together. Finally she arranged to ask for a pass over New Year, and I left her, hoping against hope that they would let her go. All was well, and after an unforgettable weekend in London I boarded the train for home.

The long tram ride from Sheffield to Handsworth, the suburb where I lived, filled me with nostalgia I found hard to acknowledge. My fellow-passengers stared at my aircrew brevet curiously, and I began to feel almost alien towards them: the plain normality of everything was so divorced from squadron life that it irritated me and I wanted to shout out, 'Don't you know what's going on out there?'

What on earth did I expect them to do? Sheffield had been bombed severely, also wartime rationing and restrictions must have made life miserable enough, yet I was glad to reach the terminus and hurry home.

My remaining leave passed swiftly. I had great admiration for my mother, now alone, keeping the home, as she put it, 'for her boys'. (My two brothers were in the Middle East, in the Navy and Army respectively.)

I met Dougie as arranged at Doncaster, and the journey to Upwood was taken up by anticipation of what to expect on our arrival. Upwood, a peace-time station, very much like Finningley where we had first formed our crew, was comfortable and well-organised. Allocated a semidetached house in the pre-war married quarters, we settled in.

It was soon obvious that training was to be concentrated mainly on navigation, so Geoff and, to a lesser degree, Bob, who would now act as second navigator, were given maximum practice, while Dougie and I contributed little.

Our first task from Upwood was a cross-country exercise of some three and a half hours' duration. The weather clamped down for the next few days, then to our amazement we were posted again, to Walboys, an airfield a few miles distant, as members of 156 Squadron Pathfinder Force.

The following day we were called to briefing for ops, and the target was again Berlin. It very much looked like learning the hard way. Our job was as Supporters to make up a reasonable number over the target while other Pathfinders were carrying out the marking. The marker bombs, carried by the experienced crews, were fitted with atmospheric fuses, set to cascade at a given height over the aiming point. They left a vivid landmark in colours that would be changed on successive raids to fox the enemy who often duplicated them in open spaces outside the target to attempt to deceive the Main Force following on.

It was no mean feat to fly over long distances at night and drop markers accurately at a given second. On the bombing run one had to fly straight and level irrespective of the opposition since wherever the markers fell those coming up behind would bomb.

Post-war historians criticised the Force for some inaccuracies. I was only a gunner, a passenger one might say, unable to influence the crew ability either way, except to do my utmost to dodge the fighters, or at least put them off by keeping alert. But I do know the effort that was put in by my own crew to arrive and bomb on time, with all possible patience, and determination not to mislead those following.

Aiming point photographs were not uncommon: losses, however, were far too high for peace of mind. In my own small way, I was proud later, as our experience mounted, to wear the PFF emblem-small, gilded metal wings, worn below the Air Crew Brevet, awarded after a probationary period and then only temporarily. The permanent award came on the issue of a certificate from the Founder and Air Officer Commanding the Force, Air Vice-Marshal D. C. T. Bennett, a brilliant pilot and navigator of vast experience.

Geoff and Bob listened carefully to the detailed briefing, for we were in exalted company, and they wanted to arrive over Berlin exactly at the same time as the crews carrying the vital target indicators.

I smiled as Tony queried, 'Who is going to support us?' on our first flight as a 'supporter'.

The prolonged flight out was strangely uneventful. I began to wonder, as we were ahead of the main force, whether the enemy fighters and their controllers had been deceived by the diversionary raids laid on by Bomber Command, and were as yet undecided and confused as to our final destination.

The flak defences seemed to be in no such doubt, and the barrage thickened by the second. There were explosions above, below and all round, as we made our run in. 'Bang on time,' I heard Geoff mutter. His ability and confidence had so much improved, that it was rare indeed from that period on for us to be off track, or more than a few seconds out on target. Bob's 'bomb doors open', as he prepared to release our load, and the city, far below beneath a near covering of cloud, now fully awakened to the threat of another holocaust, filled me with the familiar dread.

I listen with the usual irritation to his voice, unshaken by the flaming chaos all around us, counting off, until 'bomb doors closed'. I wince and press back against the turret doors, as flak bursts all around me, and a marker aircraft ahead bursts into wild conflagration as his target indicators stream down. At last we enter the wall of darkness and, looking back, I can see the brilliant red pyrotechnics as more Pathfinders release their loads.

Into the cloud that is a godsend, turning on to course for home, the weather appalling, the Lancaster shuddering and undulating, ice breaking away in fragments.

Out into the black void again, every turn of the propellers taking us nearer salvation and away from the clutches of the lurking fighters. Re-entering the cloud, with static electricity darting back and forth from the exposed gun muzzles, I crouch there and wonder if our aircraft really could explode because of this phenomenon.

The hours pass, always the constant searching, side to side, standing up again and again to peer below, ever alert, expecting streams of tracer any second from an enemy my staring eyes had failed to see.

Crossing the coast of England, the voice of the WAAF controller from distant base answering the skipper's request for a heading, finally hearing the magic words 'full flap', and the engineer calling out the airspeed, until touch down, turret locked astern, and we are back to live another day.

Just before lunch the following morning, I heard we were down for ops again that night, the first time we were to operate two nights in succession. Much less fearful now, feeling almost a veteran, I joined the crew for briefing, a more complicated affair with PFF. The various categories and functions were minutely detailed to the crews who would be marking the target blind with the use of H2S, the airborne radar that reflected the terrain below on to a cathode ray tube in the navigator's compartment, enabling him accurately to fix an aiming point completely covered by cloud.

The target was Magdeburg, a seven hour trip, for which our crew would act again as 'supporters'. I remember the calmness with which I contemplated another op so soon, but whether the experience of the previous night had bolstered my courage was uncertain: probably my mind had not had time to build up the nervous anticipation which longer lapses between ops were prone to do.

In contrast, our wireless operator confided his fears to me. 'Bugger this for a lark,' he complained as we waited at dispersal. 'Bloody PFF.' Dougie seemed inclined to agree. 'I'm knackered as it is, without going again tonight,' he proclaimed. Tony, undaunted as always, remarked that at least we should have a night off when we got back.

'When we get back,' I thought, as I connected my oxygen and heater. They were words I superstitiously disliked before the start of any operation. This would be our seventh. Could we possibly be so lucky indefinitely? Apart from our first venture to Berlin, we had received no serious damage, no deliberate, determined, attack by a night fighter. (If I had known what was to take place that very night, perhaps I would have had a different viewpoint).

Again we had little to report until nearing Magdeburg. We were too early, and Geoff called for a dog-leg to waste a little time. Dog-legs were akin to descending blind through cloud, as far as I was concerned, leaving me in constant dread, because the manoeuvre entailed cutting across the miles-wide bomber stream at forty-five degrees for a given period, then returning to the original position before resuming the prescribed course. The change of collision therefore multiplied. Even though we were ahead of the main force, there would still be other PFF aircraft in our vicinity.

I felt the pressure as we banked steeply to starboard and took the first leg, then a resounding bump and much buffeting as we crossed the slip stream of another aircraft, leaving me petrified, my eyes staring wildly, unable to pick out anything in any direction.

Soon our navigator's voice indicated the change of course, to return across the bomber stream. Without any warning, as we turned to port, an enormous black shape passed overhead impossibly near. A yell from Dougie: 'Jesus Christ – did you see that?' The next second my head was pressed up to the dome roof of the turret, as the skipper flung the Lancaster into a dive, and another huge shape slid by.

I breathed again as Geoff, cursing the loss of his instruments, was interrupted by our pilot, telling Dougie off for his useless warning. I felt guilty myself at my inability to offer any instructions for evasive action, yet – if I had – the few seconds that encompassed the whole incident would surely have made a warning superfluous. I remained silent, trying to recover my wits, nervously endeavouring to cover all the blackness around me, rotating the turret from side to side, side to side, constantly.

A brief discussion on the intercom, as no one could actually see the target, which had been usually so brightly lit when we were members of the main force, led to further speculation that we were still early. Geoff, however, was adamant that we should shortly begin the run up.

Not a sign of flak disturbed the night sky as we thundered on: it was as if they were waiting below with bated breath, unwilling to show any resistance in case they revealed that we were almost above the frightened city, covered as it was by cloud. Then the flares started to go down to starboard, to hang uniformly below, showing gaps in the cloud that lit up underneath for a brief moment, as another invisible aircraft dropped its bombs.

Indicators started to fall as we lined up for the run in. I had a glimpse of our cookie falling away as I stood up to look below, turning over and over, ungainly, unstreamlined, like an outsized oil drum. I sat down hurriedly as the flak came up as if ordered by a single command, filling the air around us with a crescendo of noise that receded into the distance as we left the awful arena, now burning brightly, a beacon for the on-coming main force that they could not miss.

A change of course, and I turned to search the blackness away from the fiery glow just in time to yell, 'Dive starboard, go!' The aircraft dropped like a stone at the skipper's instant reaction, and a stream of tracer lazily curled towards me, to zip overhead as the twin-engined fighter broke away.

Losing him for a second, I heard Dougie's Brownings, and watched the tracer hosing out and away at the enemy aircraft, which was now turning in again. I called for him to watch the port side and, quite inexplicably calm, awaited the right moment to give the instruction to evade.

Seconds before our aircraft again fell out of the sky, I pressed the firing buttons, adjusting for deviation as the tracer streamed out in a prolonged burst, then we were going down, and I was lifting from my seat, to feel the reverse pressure as the skipper wrenched her back on even keel. Utterly disoriented, I could not see the enemy; nor could Dougie find him, since our pilot was corkscrewing the aircraft constantly, port to starboard in violent evasive action, until finally reverting to the gentle weaving which he followed almost continuously when over enemy territory.

It had been a lucky escape, and fortunate that I had seen the enemy at that moment leaving the target, but even then I could not rest, and searched everywhere, my eyes leaden and watering, unable to accept that he was not still there, awaiting the opportunity to attack again.

As we descended over the North Sea, reaction set in. Infinitely weary, I puffed gratefully on my cigarette, taking the smoke deep into my lungs. The slight resultant giddiness was intoxicating and immeasurably soothing.

We landed, and there were congratulations all round. Already we were becoming welded into a formidable inter-reliant team, and every new experience only served to enhance our confidence in each other.

Visual Markers

For the next three weeks we flew cross-country exercises, some of long duration, both by day and night, mostly H2S navigation practices, which gave a respite for the gunners but hard work for our navigator, and his assistant, the bomb-aimer observer.

I caught up with my correspondence, writing long letters to Tina whom I missed so much. Letters now were much briefer to Anne, who asked me to try for leave as she had seven days to come, and whose letters to me grew more and more petulant, until I was at last informed that there was little point in continuing our relationship and that she was associating with a sub-lieutenant in Portsmouth. I imagined how pleased her father would be, and I was unperturbed.

Nights out in Peterborough, escapades that now appear childish and not a little irresponsible, 'borrowing' any mode of transport to return to base after the last bus had long gone, from bicycles to a thirty-two seater coach, which we left in the vicinity of the airfield, to be recovered by the long-suffering constabulary the next day. High spirits and hangovers, anything going in our world where the next op could mean the end of it all, and for which the RAF expression 'round the bend' was particularly apt. Yet no real harm was done or intended. Before any operation there was no drinking, ever, to my knowledge, and though discipline may have been lax on the ground, in the air there was total commitment. Not to ensure survival, for no one.

could do that. With statistics showing odds of two to one, then sooner or later you would not return. But to be certain in the knowledge that confidence in your fortitude and ability had not been misplaced by your fellow crew members.

On the surface there was little gloom or despondency, even when familiar faces disappeared from our midst;

replacements such as we had been were soon assimilated, new friends, new personalities, some irrepressible, any line-shooting greeted with laughter and light-hearted banter.

A gunner friend of mine delighted in telling outrageous stories of his crew's experiences over Germany. In one of these he solemnly related that their aircraft, coned over the target by a dozen searchlights, flew anti-clockwise in tight circles, which were followed by the Germans closely until all the bulbs in the enemy lights unscrewed. Although he with his crew did not survive, I like to imagine, whatever befell him, that his optimistic and carefree exuberance never left him to the end. He above all was sorely missed at a time when one studiously ignored the missing.

To be down for ops again after such an interlude stirred the familiar apprehensions. And now our probationary period was at an end.

Our navigator's proficiency had been proved, and we were designated for a trip to Leipzig as visual backers-up; that was to ensure that the aiming point was maintained after the primary marking had been carried out.

Briefing, as always, was long and complicated, both Geoff and Bob, acting now as second navigator in addition to his duties as bomb aimer, taking down copious notes as their section leaders emphasised every vital detail. Weather reports indicated that we could expect adverse conditions. Timing again would be of the utmost importance, any change in wind direction or speed must be noted and allowed for, and radioed back by Tobin, to be rebroadcast for the benefit of crews following on behind.

There were comparatively few instructions for the gunners' benefit: intense fighter activity could now always be expected as the enemy were gaining the upper hand, and our losses mounting at each operation. Statistically, this would have resulted in the complete loss of Bomber Command in that horrific winter 1943/44 if replacements had not been to hand, the crews and aircraft readily available. But the stark fact was that the equivalent of the whole Command was eliminated, the vast majority due to the incessant and determined efforts of enemy fighters aided by control from an efficient ground organisation. The use of 'window' (dropping bundles of metallic strips to confuse the enemy by blanketing their radar receivers) was wearing thin, inasmuch as the Germans introduced means to combat it, but we continued to use 'window', as did the aircraft on diversionary raids, to give the impression that their smaller force was the mainstream of our attack.

On this raid Berlin was to be the spoof target, and as Geoff gave the change of course, just before we reached the capital city to begin our approach to Leipzig, some of our aircraft did in fact overshoot in that direction, and the flak came up from the massed anti-aircraft guns of the defenders.

The flak over Leipzig itself was some of the worst we had encountered, and I recoiled in horror at seeing several of our aircraft go down in flames. A Halifax, slightly below, lost its complete tail assembly from a direct hit. I watched fascinated, to see the front half turn over and over, without any sign of flames or further disintegration, and with none of its crew vacating the gyrating hulk, which a moment before had flown serenely on below us, on its run-up to the aiming point.

Our run-up completed, we again reached the protection of the surrounding darkness and set course for the coast. Looking back I could see more aircraft in flames amongst the dreadful panorama of massed anti-aircraft fire that had now reached a crescendo.

Flares, high up above me, released by a night fighter, wrenched my fascinated gaze away from the receding target area, as with over-reaction I anxiously rotated the turret.

Over the sea again, I seemed to see the torment of the Halifax, that could have so easily been us, and was glad of the tiny compartment in which I sat, cramped but warm, safe and solid beneath my feet. I looked forward to the return to base and all it promised-another night out, Tina's voice, my family, and respite until the next time. At that moment I was unafraid, allowing the glad belief to invade my outraged mind that, although unable to look to the future with any certainty, we were going to make it back this night.

The following day I sat in the ante-room in the Mess reading the newspapers, and saw a large photograph on one front page which depicted a seven-man crew about to climb up into the fuselage of a Lancaster under the caption: 'Seven gentlemen bound for Berlin'. The plunging half of the Halifax from the previous night filled my mind and I stirred uneasily in the armchair. Seventy-eight of our aircraft failed to return, came the news, and I tried to imagine seventy-eight bombers lined up on the ground. They were the highest losses of the air war to date.

Tobin nudged my arm as he took the adjoining chair. 'We're on again tonight, Smithy,' he said. I put the paper down: there would be no night out tonight after all.

Before walking down to briefing, I managed to get through a 'phone call to Tina at Wickenby by using the box outside the airfield. It was good to hear her voice and reassurances that she was missing me. I told her we had operated the previous night, and she was worried and appalled at the losses incurred. I did not, of course, mention that we were on again that very evening, and if she guessed as much, as after all her duties involved airfield control, she did not indicate as much. We discussed our forthcoming leave. I gave her the date at the month-end when we hoped to get ten days and I was delighted to hear there was every possibility of our spending it together.

In an afterthought, I pushed the idea to the back of my mind. There were so many imponderables: how many ops might come up in the days between now and then? Nor did the vagaries of Service life encourage me to believe our leaves could really coincide. I longed for them to do so, yet I could not accept it as fact. In any case, we were operating that night, and this was fact enough to dominate the immediate future.

The target Stuttgart would certainly be a change from our previous sorties, in direction and time in the air. Over six hours, and later ops to this target could take even longer, depending on the route taken. We were to act again as visual backers-up, with a load consisting of flares and target indicators. Some hope was expressed that the weather would leave the target area clear.

A diversionary raid by a small force to the north was expected to draw off enemy fighters, because the spate of recent ops had been in that direction. It was anticipated that the enemy controllers would be deceived into believing that a repeat attack was going in, similar to the raid on Leipzig of the previous evening.

Feeling physically tired, I settled down in the familiar surroundings of the turret, which I had vacated only twenty-four hours earlier. Becoming drowsy, as R for Robert climbed laboriously into the evening sky, I turned down the heating, but the symptoms persisted, and a check on the oxygen supply proved no fault. Before we crossed the enemy coast, I slipped a 'wakey-wakey' tablet into my mouth, feeling the bitter taste on my tongue. I was glad of it, and soon became wide-eyed and alert. The previous drowsiness I blamed on the mental exertions of the previous night. (Total flying hours for the two consecutive ops were thirteen hours twenty-five minutes.)

We pressed on undisturbed, and it began to look as if our planners had really scored with their deceptions. After marking the target on time, we left the city well ablaze, with opposition only slight, compared with our sorties to Berlin and Leipzig. Circling base on return, before our landing approach, I was just congratulating myself that it had all been a piece of cake when I had cause to give instruction for evasive action, as another Lancaster came hurtling towards us out of nowhere. It was a very near miss, and I could hear the skipper, as he straightened out, cursing at the 'sonofabitch' who had crossed the circuit at right angles and almost caused a collision. When I received a verbal pat on the back from him in dispersal later, I felt a little guilty, for just before sighting the offending Lancaster I had been idly watching below, impatiently waiting our call with permission to land, and it had been pure chance that, looking up, I had sighted the other aircraft. I vowed then that I would never relax until we were down. It was another lesson learned.

CHAPTER SIX

Collision Course

It was late when I awoke the following day after a sleep of exhaustion. Obviously no ops for us that night, and after a good meal in the back room of the local pub in Ramsey, we had a glorious session, half carrying, half dragging Tobin to the airfield, much the worse for wear. His annoyance the next day to find the toes of his best shoes almost worn away only fuelled our laughter.

It was about this time that I became acquainted with a Flight Sergeant rear gunner, who with his crew had recently joined the Squadron. He seemed to be a quiet introvert, and I had been intrigued to learn that he had already completed his first tour of ops in Stirlings. This was an aircraft I had only been near once-during our OTU course at Finningley, when we had forced landed at Waterbeach in our Wellington. Then, the sheer size of the Stirling had astonished me, although now, with the predominance of the Lancaster, it could be considered obsolete.

After a few drinks had loosened his tongue one evening, Bill related some of his experiences. It appeared that, nearing the end of his first tour, his pilot had suffered some injury returning from operations to Frankfurt. To his and his crew's dismay, the remaining ops to complete their tour had been undertaken firstly by a Flight Commander as skipper, and finally, on the last one, by a pilot whose competence left a lot to be desired. All this had unnerved him at the time. Worse was to come, however, for after the rest period as an instructor he had been crewed up with a comparatively new crew and posted to Upwood for training with the Pathfinder Force.

After two trips over Germany, he was convinced that his present skipper was unable to cope: he had already shown signs of panic on several occasions when things had got a bit rough over the other side. Although it was obvious that Bill did not want to go on, he could not very well refuse point-blank to fly, and he was unwilling to ask for a transfer. How I sympathised with his predicament: the idea of operating with anyone other than my own crew appalled me, and not to have absolute confidence in one's pilot didn't bear thinking about.

All I could do was to express my condolences, and lamely put forward the opinion that perhaps his skipper would gain confidence with experience, while acknowledging to myself how infantile my remarks were. Admittedly everyone had to start somewhere, and our own experiences had been horrific, yet we had faced them as a close-knit team. Furthermore we had flown together from the beginning, and each crisis had only improved our co-operation and confidence in each other.

I could understand Bill's apprehension, but at the back of my mind, I wondered if perhaps he had been prejudiced by his experience, or that long absence from operational flying had unnerved him.

All that remained to be seen. Later I was to meet his skipper on numerous occasions, and as a fellow Yorkshireman I made a point of starting conversations with him, he of course being unaware of his rear gunner's confidences to me. I frequently noticed his reluctance to discuss his operations over Germany. Bill made no more comments, but as time went on I noticed his preoccupation at briefings, as if in isolation, how quiet and almost noncommittal he had become in the Mess, and his drinking when not scheduled for ops, becoming excessive. I disclosed none of my knowledge or misgivings to anyone, even though Bill's habits were becoming a source of some comment. His torment left me disquieted and apprehensive.

My constant enquiries to our skipper about the date of our expected leave brought the usual uncomplimentary remarks from the crew: 'Randy bugger' and 'You wouldn't have a clue what to do anyway' amongst the many. That Tina's leave had now been confirmed left me almost

Air Vice-Marshal Donald Bennett, CB, CBE, DSO.

Air Vice-Marshal D.C.T. Bennett CB CBE DSO, leader of the Pathfinder Force (centre)
photographed at 156 Squadron, RAF Warboys with (left) W/Cdr. T.L. Bingham-Hall
DFC (later G/Capt DSO DFC) Squadron Commander, and Group Captain J.L. Airey DFC,
Station Commander.

Squadron Leader Jack Cuthill, DSO, DFC,
pilot of Ron Smith's aircraft.

Group Captain
T.G. Mahaddie,
DSO, DFC, AFC & bar

Aircrew and ground crew of 156 Squadron surrounding their Pathfinder chief, Air Vice-Marshal Bennett, and their Station and their Station and Squadron Commander.

RAF Upwood August 1944 – 2nd tour of ops. finnished. Members of two crews. Back: Unknown. Middle: Bert Wilson W/Op, Jack Watson Flt Eng., Weston Appleby Mid-Upper. Front: Doug Aspinall Mid-Upper, Ron Smith Rear Gunner.

Ron Smith DFM

distraught. I had expected that she would have the problems, not I. Then as the last few days passed without further briefing, my hopes soared until, on the 24th February, we were down to operate. I cursed the powers that be and joined the crew at briefing.

A strategic attack on Schweinfurt in Southern Germany, to eliminate the vital ball-bearing factories, was, we were informed, vital. If the raid was unsuccessful we would have to repeat the operation. Our role on this occasion was as supporters. The target area, it was suggested, should be clear, and extra efforts were called for from the experienced, primary marker crews to find the aiming point visually. An unusual aspect of the planning was that the aircraft involved would be split up into two distinct waves, with a two-hour interval between each.

I was pleased to hear that we would be foremost in the first attack, which seemed preferable to the second wave, although some advantage might be gained there if the fighters were re-fuelling after intercepting the first attack. There was the further possibility that the enemy controllers would hardly expect a second attack so soon on the same night.

Again I dismissed all thought of the anticipated leave from my mind: to be going on ops was sufficiently thought-provoking without other distractions.

Thirty-three aircraft were lost that night, two of which were from our Squadron. I could see the target from a great distance as we made our way homeward. I imagined the second wave going in as we were returning, and decided that they would find navigation easy, with the target a beacon against the night sky.

We landed and taxied to dispersal without incident, after being airborne for seven and three-quarter hours, and the general opinion at debriefing was that it had been a good trip with considerable success.

The following evening saw us outward bound for Augsburg and I was beginning to think that there was a conspiracy afoot to prevent us ever going on leave again. Personally, although disgruntled and tired after the long haul of the previous night, I settled down in the turret confidently. Whether the trouble-free trip to Schweinfurt had made me complacent, I don't know, but even approaching the enemy coast failed to dispel my equanimity.

Cloud cover was patchy and it looked as if the meteorological forecast was accurate. Our function over the target was again as supporters, carrying a mixed load of bombs and incendiaries.

Augsburg housed a Messerschmitt aircraft works and I was surprised that the flak was comparatively light over such an important target. Whether it was because we were one of the first aircraft in, I'm not sure, but nothing untoward happened as our load went down. Glancing down, I could see the outline of the town below, streets and buildings standing out clearly, fires starting to take hold. Indicators streamed down as the Pathfinders found the aiming point.

As we banked away on the course for home, a sudden yell from Dougie, giving instructions to 'dive port go'. A stream of tracer came from above and behind me, as the skipper responded immediately, and the aircraft dropping sickeningly made me duck involuntarily, any complacency disappearing in a second.

As we came out of the dive and began to climb, I saw a Junkers 88 banking at an incredible angle, to come in again slightly below, clearly discernible against the floodlit target area. I had no time to wonder at his folly as I gave him a long burst that appeared to pass right through him, with some rounds deflecting off in all directions, before down we went in a violent corkscrew.

For a few minutes I watched the enemy, now on our port quarter up, flying along with us yet out of range. The crew were silent while I gave a constant running commentary to keep the skipper informed.

The Junkers pilot's tactics made me wonder if he had a

partner with him, who might attack from starboard. Dougie was watching this area from his vantage position, as I kept my eyes glued on the persistent enemy. For a brief moment I tried to convince myself that perhaps our reactions up to then had put him off, only to see him turn in again at some distance to approach from immediately behind, when normally he could have been expected to come in at an angle and not line up behind until near breakaway. A fighter with fixed guns must aim ahead of his target, and if his adversary turns into his angle of attack at the right moment, he normally cannot maintain his aim, and breaks off the attack, which is a good time to return his fire when his aircraft is most vulnerable.

My problem, therefore, was if I gave evasive action too soon he could adjust and follow, so I prepared the skipper for a corkscrew and gave the approaching menace a long burst, even though at maximum range for my Brownings. As he opened fire the tracer seemed to come straight at me. I gave the instruction to 'Go', and as we went down on the first part of the manoeuvre his tracer passed overhead well away, not as I supposed directly at me. I immediately lost sight of him. We came up, to dive again on the second leg of the corkscrew, my skipper's action precise but violent enough to pin me to my seat by the centrifugal force.

Dougie had opened fire when I did, and he said that the Junkers had broken away to our port below but, as the skipper weaved from side to side, nothing could be seen, no outline against the blackness, no patch darker than the surrounding void.

As I turned the turret restlessly to starboard, the whole sky lit up in an instant behind me, and our aircraft banked away at our pilot's reaction. I turned the turret to port against the pressure, in time to see a Lancaster falling to the ground below, other bombers here and there, flying steadily on, as if awaiting their execution passively. Still no glimpse of the enemy, as again the blackness closed in all round, only the distant glow far below where our comrades had fallen. Soon this was to disappear, and eventually we crossed the enemy coast, the defences trying one last fling before we escaped. The flak flickered up all along the perimeter, some at a great distance, to spark out as the blessed Merlins took us on and away from the torment behind.

A small thread hanging from my helmet touched my face and I jumped and pulled my head away violently, nerves raw, body numb with fatigue. The repeated attacks by the Junkers had been short-lived, my comments on tactics an afterthought, for in the few seconds of the enemy approach there was little time to think. His last attempt had been unusual in being so easily seen. It made me wonder whether the pilot felt contempt for our defences, which were so puny in comparison with the armament of the American Flying Fortress.

Back at base we learned that one of our aircraft had not returned, and nothing was heard, then or later of their fate. I thought about the blazing Lancaster near Augsburg -that too had been a supporter.

Much to our delight our skipper received his promotion to Flight Sergeant on the following day, and we celebrated the event at the local that night. There was as yet no news of our leave, and we spent two days of the month on practice bombing and fighter affiliation, when a Spitfire made repeated attacks from all angles while we practised the appropriate evasive action.

Tina rang to say that her leave commenced on the last Saturday of the month, and asking me to ring her at home in York as soon as I could get away. She sounded a little edgy when I could not specify the date, and so was I, for we should, and normally would, have known when leave was due. It appeared that Tina's widowed mother was ill, and our plans to spend a few days at a cottage they owned, near Ullswater in the Lake District, were in jeopardy. As I replaced the receiver, after promising to ring the first moment I could with any news, I felt a surge of disappointment at the break-up of our plans.

The remainder of the crew were also complaining, and the skipper promised to find out what he could. He returned with the unexpected news that the whole Squadron was to move back to Upwood, and that the training unit for PFF would take over at Warboys. This impending move had been the cause of the uncertainty about our leave. We were to be on ops again that night, but our leave would commence the following day. Accepting the information with mixed feelings I decided to ring Tina on our return.

A repeat attack on Stuttgart, visited some ten days previously, was outlined at briefing. Designated as blind backers-up again, we paid strict attention to the detail of the extended route, which would entail a flight time for the trip of seven and a half hours.

Considering the number of turning points, as we feinted our way out to the target, we reached the run up to the aiming point almost uneventfully. There, a discussion between Geoff and Bob took place as to the accuracy of our approach, which ended in some disagreement. Certainly, the target indicators I could see were widespread and not at all concentrated. However, I was grateful to hear 'Bomb doors closed' as Bob released our load and we turned on course for the distant French coast.

The return journey from this raid stands out in my memory. As I recall it, even now, so many years afterwards, my inability to prevent what happened remains. Nearing the French coast visibility improved markedly, so much so that I could see quite plainly a Lancaster in all detail slightly below, moving slowly across our course. Then, as I moved the turret in the other direction, another Lancaster could be observed, equally plainly, sliding almost imperceptibly across the other's path. As they edged nearer each other, as if intending to formate side by side, I eased the turret dead astern, so that both aircraft were now centred in my view.

As they were of no direct concern to us, I was about to rotate the turret away to one side, in my search for the enemy, when I noticed that they were still closing the gap, narrowing the distance between them. I still expected they would pass one above the other, for in the time it took to make their approach, in such visibility, it was beyond my comprehension that they had not observed each other. Suddenly, I realised the truth, and shouted out a useless warning.

Then a mighty eruption, a fountain of flame and falling debris, the night air all around us as day, our own aircraft falling away, the skipper fighting for control as the blast all but turned us over.

I tried to explain what I had seen as we resumed our course. All of us were badly shaken, and 1, who had a grandstand seat over a boundless arena, had witnessed the unbelievable – two superb aircraft and fourteen highly trained aircrew eliminated, colliding in conditions of perfect visibility.

I banged my gloved fist in sheer impotence on the gun mounting. 'Why? Why?' I asked out loud, with only the continued roar of our own engines to answer me. All the way to base I could not rest or relax. As we circuited, awaiting our turn to land, my mind kept asking over and over again, why, oh why had they not seen each other? I put the question repeatedly to the crew as we ate our meal after de-briefing, but it was a useless inquest.

Later, in that brief moment before exhaustion closed my mind in sleep, I watched again those two aircraft closing below, mentally to sound my useless warning, sickened and disgusted at the waste of war. Still tired and irritable, I rang Tina, who told me she was expecting her aunt to stay with her mother for a few days. I promised to pick her up at her home the following day, and caught the train in Peterborough to Sheffield to spend that night with my mother. As the train gathered speed and the countryside swept by I knew beyond all doubt that I could never leave those memories behind.

Just before the war, my father had been fortunate enough to win some two hundred and fifty pounds (in those days a considerable amount) with an Irish Sweepstake ticket. Although unable to drive himself he had purchased a small second-hand car, a Singer Bantam and my brother and I had delighted in learning to drive it. When we joined the Forces, the vehicle was put on blocks and left in the garage at home.

I managed eventually to start it, after the battery had been charged. Despite rationing, the local garage filled it up with petrol and with some persuasion gave me a couple of cans as well. Without tax or insurance I set off hopefully, the Bantam chugging along nicely, to pick up Tina and take her to the Lake District. As we progressed along the country lanes, I prayed the old car would not let me down: I had looked forward so much to the few days alone with my girl-friend, and the very thought that something would spoil it all kept me on tenterhooks, listening for any false note from the engine, and muttering to myself, 'I don't give a damn as long as you get me there.'

Before reaching York I managed to scrounge more petrol, my uniform softening the heart of a formidable looking garage owner, and after numerous enquiries found Tina's address at the end of a terrace, in a quiet backwater north of the city. Anxiously I waited for a reply to my knocking, hoping against hope that her mother's health had improved, selfishly concerned that our plans might come to nought.

All was well. Tina's aunt was present, her mother's health much better, and Tina herself looking marvellous in civilian clothes. She was all ready to go, and although her mother was a little wary she offered no objections to our going away together. Her aunt, however, looked distinctly disapproving.

More petrol in Penrith, and we finally reached the cottage at Ullswater. Tina had related on the journey how her aunt's objections to her going away with me had aroused her mother's doubts. These, however, she had finally overcome, and her main concern was what her aunt would be saying in her absence.

Our superb surroundings, the walks, our amateur efforts

at fishing, the excitement when I actually caught one, and the evenings in the pub, made our stay unforgettable. The experience gave me a deep and lasting love, which remains to this day, for that part of our country. Over the years I have, when able to afford it, escaped to this unspoiled haven to explore and rejoice in the words that Wordsworth wrote, in total understanding.

> *Remote from public road or dwelling,*
> *Pathway, or cultivated land;*
> *From trace of human foot or hand.*
> *There sometimes doth a leaping fish*
> *Send through the tarn a lonely cheer;*
> *The crags repeat the raven's croak,*
> *In symphony austere;*
>
> *'Fidelity'*

Rising often at dawn to stand beside the quiet lake which reflected the hills and trees in the early light, envying the bard's ability to describe all this with such wonderful economy of words, was to be on another planet, another world, a million miles removed...

Here, in peace untouched, undisturbed by the sounds of war, I found a faith in my Maker, that hitherto had only become profound when in mortal danger, or anxiety. Here with a heart and mind, I tried to grapple with the knowledge that for these few days I had been allowed through a gate in the wall which divided this heaven from my existence in the unreal realities of squadron life.

Tina was as reluctant to return as I was, although she was anxious about her mother. However, when my gallant little car pulled up outside her home late on the Friday night we found her mother continuing to improve, and her aunt (after accepting a small present) more amenable.

Congratulating myself on my deceitful diplomacy, I left a tearful Tina, promising to take her away on my next leave if she could co-ordinate hers at the same time, although we were inclined to doubt this, as the operational leave allowance meant that I was receiving seven days every six weeks now.

I met Dougie at Doncaster the following day, and as our crowded train steamed out of the busy station, making its way south, I idly watched a Wellington bomber passing overhead, reminding me of the days at Finningley which seemed so long ago. As I nodded off to sleep, the rhythm of the train's wheels increased their monotonous tempo, seeming to delight in ignoring my reluctance to return.

CHAPTER SEVEN

Nuremberg

The squadron losses were now becoming prohibitive, the atmosphere in the Mess, subdued. Among all the new faces that abounded, it was going to take time to settle in again. The next day we transferred to Upwood on a fifteen minute flight. I watched the Lancasters land one after the other, to be allocated their dispersal's.

It was like the assembling of a new squadron, in the new environment of a peace-time airfield, with its permanent buildings and married quarters surrounded by trim lawns. The Mess, too, was on a par with the other facilities and everyone seemed cheered by the transfer. After a practice bombing exercise that afternoon, a WAAF party was well attended, and we settled in our semi-detached, pre-war married quarters reasonably comfortably.

Ops were on the following day, our crew were promoted to be Blind Marker Illuminators, and the target was the now familiar Stuttgart. That we had been allocated a spare aircraft because our beloved R for Robert was unserviceable did not serve to put me in a confident mood as we reached dispersal. I eyed the aircraft with distrust: the turret, although identical, transmitted that temporary feeling. These were not my guns, and I was superstitious enough to allow some unease to develop as we taxied out for take-off.

I need not have been so concerned. The seven and a half hour trip was one of the most uneventful we had yet attempted, and although our run-up to the aiming point had its complications the weather did not encourage any attempt by fighters to find us. We returned through intermittent cloud, weary, yet with nothing extraordinary to report. We were to hear later that the marking was poor and widespread, much to the disgust of Geoff, who insisted that we had marked on time and in the right spot, and he was supported by Bob, who had released the indicators.

Two successive ops to Frankfurt followed, and we became established in our role as Blind Markers. The second sortie resulted in our obtaining an aiming-point photograph, for which we enthusiastically congratulated Geoff and Bob.

The increasing efficiency of our crew, the constant training on air exercises between ops and our immunity from attack on the last three raids, did not conspire to make me over-confident, although, as we took our seats at briefing on the day after our success at Frankfurt, a touch of arrogance could be detected, as again we were to operate as Blind Markers. The next trip, however, a maximum effort on our old enemy Berlin, introduced the familiar butterflies in the stomach, as I visualised the long nerve-wracking vigil over the heart of Germany, and the prolonged run across the huge expanse of the capital with its mass defences.

I was grateful that R-Robert was available again and I looked around affectionately, feeling more at home in the turret that had witnessed so many of my past experiences.

It wasn't very long after we had left the enemy coast behind on our outward journey that Geoff could be heard telling Bob that the forecast wind was so inaccurate that he could hardly believe his own calculations. These were vital if we were to stay on track, and it was only after rechecking, and with confirmation from Bob, that Geoff decided that his own figures were correct. Even so, his exclamations continued to express astonishment at the calculated velocities until we reached the target. The airborne radar H2S, however, confirmed his persistence, and our red indicators went down on time.

As we left the target area, flak burst directly below with stunning violence, and I froze as we lost height alarmingly. The starboard outer engine was back-firing, the skipper and Tony juggling with the controls, until finally, with the engine feathered and useless, we turned anxiously on the long haul back to the coast. I searched the night sky constantly as we plodded on and on, while frequent adjustments to our heading were being made meticulously by Geoff. His voice became irritable, as first Dougie and then I asked him, 'How far to the coast?'

Flak was coming up at some distance on both sides, and searchlights further afield were active. I could tell from this that the weather had dispersed the bomber stream, and that many aircraft were overflying the heavily-defended area of the Ruhr. Time and time again, I saw the ghastly spectacle of our comrades falling from the sky like flaming comets as the concentrated flak took its toll.

I could imagine the reactions of the new crews, with inexperienced navigators, being blown way off course by the freak weather, and I listened with admiration as Geoff competently gave the last heading for home. Once there, we were given priority to land, because of the feathered engine. Our safe return was another superb effort by our imperturbable skipper.

Next morning the damage was obvious: the engine nacelle and surrounding wing surfaces had been pockmarked and made ragged by the near direct hit.

Seventy-eight aircraft failed to return, three from our own squadron. 'Seventy-eight,' I repeated to myself as I made my way to the gunnery section. How long would the God of chance smile upon us? Even if we continued with all the expertise in the world, a direct hit, such as we had just avoided, would have sent us careering down with negligible chances of survival.

There were no ops for us that night, though some squadron crews were operating. We decided by a majority vote to spend the evening in the Mess. I for one did not fancy the bus journey into Peterborough, and it was in sombre mood that we walked across the grass to see our friends depart, to wish them well, and to hope that the target was a comparatively easy one. Darkness was settling down over the airfield as I stood with others at the runway, awaiting the first heavily-laden aircraft to run up to full power for take off.

One after the other the Lancasters moved forward, identical in form and power, yet each controlled by seven individuals, seven hearts and minds, each with his own personality, fears and aspirations.

As the last shadowy silhouette lifted into the dusky air, the crowd of sightseers dispersed slowly, their voices hardly audible against the swelling volume of a multitude of engines, rolling and thundering overhead as if to crush the very mind beneath the weight of sound.

I stayed for some minutes, refusing the invitations to return to the Mess, and walked slowly away along the now vacated circle of the perimeter track. The sound of my footsteps on the concrete gradually became audible as the receding sound of the engines allowed the evening air some respite. At intervals appeared the vague outlines of vacant dispersal's, awaiting the return of their occupants, the silence broken only by the last calls of birds settling for the night, no longer in competition with the man-made tumult, their fellows answering from beyond the boundary fence, hidden in the darkness which now cloaked the countryside. I quickened my pace, as if to forestall the ever-present mode of existence from pervading my mind for this brief moment, happy to be alone, unwilling to allow the fractions to come together. Yet the problem remained. Will I survive? And what is the experience doing to my mind? My life pre-war had not prepared me for this, nor had the love and affection I had known at home.

The familiar beat of Merlin engines stopped me in my tracks, to stand and listen intently. The distant throb became a constant roar, as the blackness gave way to a glow strung across the airfield, the runway lights spacing out the distance. A change in the engines' note as the pitch altered for landing, the dark shape winking out the lights temporarily, showing its slowing progress as the engines cut to the backfire of exhausts.

Some crew had returned after aborting the raid, as we had

done so long ago it seemed, at Wickenby. The spell was broken. I changed direction, cutting across the grass in a direct line towards the Mess to join the others at the bar.

The Lancaster lay quiet at dispersal, the voices of the crew faint in the distance.

The birds made no sound.

By March 30th 1944, I had completed sixteen operations, three in the preceding ten days, and the squadron's catastrophic losses had been made up again by replacement crews from the PFF Training Unit down the road at Warboys. None was without experience and quite a number were on second tours. There was little out of the ordinary about this particular day of squadron routine, although there had been the usual flap on as ops were announced for that evening, and some comment at briefing when the route to the target revealed an unusually long leg, without any deviation, direct to Nuremberg from a point near the Belgian-German frontier.

True, we had not operated to Nuremberg before, but a number of ops in that direction to Schweinfurt and Augsburg had been our lot, and although our target that night was some distance further south, no particular alarm, other than the usual pre-op nerves, troubled my mind as we dressed before being driven out to our aircraft. Yet this raid, and its disastrous consequences, will remain in the annals of Bomber Command as the cross-roads at which a complete reappraisal of the whole strategy of our offensive was to be undertaken.

There have been many arguments since then, in remarkable books written by participants, and in dry official versions, which have apportioned the blame. I read them avidly, and I know which views I accept-those of the people who were there. But throughout this whole narrative my only endeavour has been to try to portray my own reactions, purely as a rear gunner, enclosed in a perspex capsule, totally isolated from the other crew; to convey my depth of feeling, devoid as far as possible from any technical appraisal on which I was not competent to offer comment then, and have no wish to research now.

My diary at the time contains the details of the mental struggle I underwent. Others like me experienced much more. It goes without saying that the contribution by pilots and navigators, with their added responsibility, was beyond all praise. The turret had become my own little world, and I offer only the view of the battle from it, perhaps with an insight into the strivings for adjustment in my mind.

As we neared the enemy coast on the interminable trip out, I was aghast at the near daylight visibility provided by a brilliant moon. Never before had I experienced such stark conditions: I could just look around and see for miles in all directions, and the patches of cloud below made us like flies, crawling across a pure white tablecloth. If that cloud had been consistent, I could have picked out any enemy fighter with ease – an advantage which did not impress me. Gone was the blessed darkness, the cloak that offered such welcome anonymity.

The intercom remained silent after the skipper's reminder to keep our eyes open, except for some apt remarks from Dougie, giving his opinion of the met. men, whose forecast, as he put it, 'Was all to cock'. Perched up there, on top of the fuselage, with such a view all around him, he must have felt infinitely more vulnerable than any of us.

It was some comfort to observe two other Lancasters as we crossed the coast, and odd to see the puffs of smoke from the exploding shells as flak came up. The flash they produced, anaemic in the moonlight, was not at all as seen against the usual pitch blackness.

It was then the tragedy unfolded, so early, as we made for the only turning point before the long leg to our target. All too often I had been a horrified witness in the past, and yet one did not become immune to seeing aircraft go down in flames.

This one was different. Initially the Lancaster furthest away from us, but plainly outlined, exploded in a welter of flames. Then the one nearer to us was also enveloped, though still flying straight and level, flames reaching back, three tiny figures only, clearly discernible, jumping out to fall away.

The enemy fighter, now breaking away below turned towards us, looking for another easy kill. I stood up, leaning as far forward as I could to peer below, while our aircraft weaved from side to side. Through my now frantic mind, the torment ran that there might be something further ahead, out of my line of sight.

Then Dougie's voice, calling instructions for evasive action, superbly timed, his Brownings firing at the same time as a JU88 broke away to my left below, the Lancaster going down with such velocity that I was pressed on top of the gun mountings and a sharp blow on the forehead leaving me dizzy with pain.

I regained my seat sick with apprehension, swallowing the vomit in my throat, turning the turret hurriedly towards a flicker of flame close by, as another aircraft mortally hit cascaded down into the misty depths.

Geoff's anxious voice gave our new course as we banked to starboard, and I counted several more victims lighting up the already flood-lit scene around us. The Germans were having a field day, they could not miss, and the awful, pitiful patches of still-burning wreckage, marked the landscape below, behind and all around.

At last a respite as we penetrated deeper into enemy territory, but a respite only in the immediate vicinity, for the night still distantly pinpointed where our comrades went down. I had tried to count but lost the figure as the dreadful total mounted. Although we were as yet unaware of the final tragic consequences of that night, it seemed obvious that, back at home, so far away and at that moment beyond reach, someone in authority had 'dropped a clanger'. This was no ordinary raid, if any could be described as such.

The long straight leg to the target at last came to an end, and we prepared for the final run-up to the Nazi show place,

Nuremberg. For the first time, our navigator's experience and intense training had resulted in our selection as prime marker illuminators.

Just as our markers went down, after a nerve-shattering straight and level approach, again we were attacked by a fighter. His intentions had been obvious – I had watched him for some time – high above on our starboard quarter. As I gave evasive instructions, I maintained pressure on the firing buttons, and all four guns responded to send him breaking away, straight down, a dwindling speck against the lurid glow below. I was convinced I had hit him, yet he hadn't broken up or burst into flame.

No damage as we turned on course for the long run home. 'Will this one never end?' was the thought running through my mind as I numbly watched four bombers go down, one after the other. 'Christ, how many is that tonight – thirty, forty, or more?' I asked myself and chewed hard on the tasteless wad of gum in my mouth. They continued to go down until at full power we streaked across the coast and out over the sea. the waves but a ripple far below. Suddenly, the weather deteriorated, dense cloud hiding all from view. From the front, Bob muttered a comment on the meteorological forecast, 'The bastards must have got it arse about.' The contrast after the hours of brilliant moonlight seemed ironical, and it was hard to believe a forecast could have been so completely wrong. If only the conditions had been reversed, how welcome this cloud would have been in the previous tragic hours!

The skipper made a distant call to base, only to be informed that the weather had closed down and that we were to divert to Downham Market, some sixty miles south-east of our own airfield. The new course was set as we began the descent. With the choice remarks of the crew in my ears, I looked wearily below. The skipper's voice, now edgy from fatigue, ordered silence. He still had the enormous responsibility of putting down safely at a strange airfield in the appalling weather that we had flown into so unexpectedly. The silence is unbroken, the heavy tension becomes more unbearable as no cloud base is reached. Other aircraft are calling for instructions, and still we descend.

I shift on the tiny hard rectangle that answers as a seat, but the cramp returns to pain my buttocks almost immediately as I resume my posture. I stand up to peer in front and below, down into murk for any sign that will indicate we have reached cloud base. Naked fear keeps the adrenaline flowing, and even after several hours my mind and body are unable to allow the drug of exhaustion to predominate.

When at last our shuddering aircraft leaves cloud, any direct contrast in visibility is not immediately noticeable. Then, as a patch below clears, I see perimeter lights astern, a runway partly revealed, the glow subdued as it reflects from the low cloud above.

A curse from the skipper at my exclamations, another call to control as we begin the circuits, going around several times as other aircraft hold the approach. Finally instructions and permission to land, the lights obscured momentarily as we pass through patches and wisps of mist.

The lengthy careful run in, a quick sight of a wooden barred fence just beneath, a sudden blur of lights and we are down, the runway unreeling before my eyes, the squeal of brakes, safe at last, after almost eight hours that swerved a lifetime.

As we await transport, I glance up at our aircraft affectionately, the sheer size of the triple-bladed propellers fronting the engine nacelles, never failing to impress me.

Incredibly, the nightmare is over, our pilot nodding only at our congratulations, undemonstrative as ever. Debriefing in unfamiliar surroundings, the intelligence officer startled by the figures we suggest of aircraft shot down.

Sleep evades me long after I crawl beneath the sheets, the engines' roar still pervading my ears, my mind a blank, unable to grapple with, or even register with clarity, any one of the multiple horrors of that awful night.

CHAPTER EIGHT

Preparation for D Day

Next morning we made the short journey to base over the English countryside, the patchwork of fields, villages, a small town, a ribbon of railway receding into the distance, a snail-like train only distinguished by the trailing smoke and steam from the miniature locomotive at its head.

Five aircraft were missing, we were informed in the flight office; total for the whole of Bomber Command was eighty, and another sixteen had crashed on return in various parts of Southern England, ninety-six in all.

Yes, someone had miscalculated, someone had got it all wrong. Although the morning promised to be fine, to develop into one of those early summer days, here before its time, the catastrophe of the previous night was hard to accept.

Ten days were to pass before ops were again announced, the interval being spent on navigational and bombing exercises, while Dougie and I got in some practical air-to-air firing at a drogue.

As we walked out to dispersal to take our new Lancaster out on air test – M for Mother – there was still a chill in the air, but with a hint of the coming spring. The quiet fields that made up the surrounding countryside were already showing green in the morning sun.

In the Gunnery Section earlier, we had been informed that some bright spark in authority had decided that, no matter how clean and polished the perspex was maintained in the rear turrets, vision was still restricted by twenty-five per cent. It had been decided therefore to cut away the perspex directly in front of the gunners, up to where it curved into the dome of the turret at the top, and also at the sides, leaving nothing between the gunner and the sky, and thus improving vision. There would be no difficulty weather-wise, as the slipstream would take care of that.

Sitting in the turret, I had mixed feelings. Perspex was anything but armour plate, but the very fact of having it in front of me had been some comfort. Now it had been removed I felt naked and exposed. Dougie grinned at me through the opening. 'You'll be able to shake hands with the bastards now, Smithy,' he laughed.

For some time rumours of the impending invasion of Europe had been widespread, and the general public could not have been more aware of the build-up of arms, men and material in the southern part of England. On air exercises we had over-flown vast camps, to see the figures of thousands of soldiers come running out as we roared low overhead. I didn't envy them their task, but I was pleased to see that the target uncovered at briefing was the marshalling yards at Le Bourget, Paris, and our first contribution to the immense undertaking of those soldiers.

Great care was to be taken to avoid French civilian casualties, and it was emphasised again and again that our markers must be spot-on tonight of all nights. I was now too old a hand to contribute wholeheartedly to the views expressed by some back at base, that this sortie would be 'a piece of cake'. The round trip of three hours fifty minutes sounded much more agreeable than 'stooging' across Germany, yet I was alert for trouble as we crossed the French coast, still all too well aware of the yawning gap that had been cut away in front of me. In the event, we were tackled by a JU88 practically all the way into the target; time after time he came in out of the semi-darkness, his cannon fire so near above and below. The lack of any protection, useless though it would have been, was uppermost in my mind as I continually rotated the turret to face him.

By the time he finally broke away, my ammunition must have been getting low and I felt bruised and battered and not a little queasy, after the almost continual evasive action. The fact remained we could not see him, and after such a persistent attack my imagination ran riot. If I searched to one side, I was certain he would be approaching from the other. Time crawled by, however, and nothing disturbed the darkness all around.

'Good show, Smithy,' said the skipper – rare praise indeed from one who did not often show his feelings.

Our target indicators went down smack in the centre of the marshalling yards, to join others already placed there, where the network of railway lines and shunting areas were clearly visible. I thought about the French people below in the famous city, of what their reaction would be, and if they were aware that their ordeal of occupation was nearly over.

In no time we were circling base, impatiently awaiting our turn to land, while caustic and rude remarks were directed over the radio telephone at any sluggard who took too much time on his landing approach. The cool impersonal WAAF voice below brought a reminder to adhere to RT procedure.

Back to Germany the next evening, to attack Cologne, the name famous since the first one-thousand bomber raid in 1942. There was no opposition on the short journey out, but just before our markers were released I looked up immediately above us, and there hovered another Lancaster with bomb-doors gaping open. I had hardly reported this to the skipper when his bombs came down, to pass close on the starboard side.

A single-engined fighter appeared and moved up towards our beam, and although I rotated the turret to its maximum ninety degrees I could not get a sight on him. As I leaned half over, trying to keep him in view, the turret doors behind me slammed wide open. I pressed forward against the guns as the slipstream, almost solid in consistency, tugged at my parachute harness.

The thought of the void behind and below me chilled me with fear. Very carefully I eased the turret astern, until my back once again was aligned with the fuselage. Try as I might I could not budge either door. I clawed desperately at it from my cramped position, and at last the port side door came free to slide across, half covering the gap. In the meantime, the fighter was maintaining his position, following us into the darkness, while I gingerly moved the turret, exposing my half-covered back. No attack came, and we followed our course home.

Nearing base my leg was pulled unmercifully, with remarks such as, 'I bet the windy bugger was going to bail out'....

Next morning the offending door was eased and seemed to lock securely without effort. I was at a loss to understand why the incident had occurred when it did, and not on the way out. From then on I always checked more thoroughly that the doors were secure, but I was loth to press back against them for some time afterwards.

Our leave came around again, and after an awkward delayed journey to Lincoln I met Tina at our rendezvous in the city centre. She had only an overnight pass, and our few hours together passed all too quickly. Whether she resented the fact that I was going home for the remainder of my week's leave I do not know but I didn't want to hang about all day to see her only in the evenings. I was feeling restless and really desired so much to get away on my own, although on the train to Sheffield I felt not a little disquieted and morose at this revelation of my deepest feelings.

The centre of Sheffield had been tidied up, but the results of the blitz with hollow skeletons of the burnt-out department stores and other buildings still showed what mass bombing could inflict on a built-up area. The sun shone along the city streets, however, and the population crowded the pavements, even though their rationed shopping must have been meagre. My strange resentment of the otherwise supreme normality of everyone and everything was once again irritating and frustrating.

Some time later, after too many beers and feeling very isolated, I boarded the slow tram for home, numbly watching the familiar scene as the long miles dragged by. I passed the little cinema I used to love to visit whenever I could scrounge the sixpence entry-fee, and the park where Easter Parades, after brightening the sad city streets, used to gather around the bandstand in its centre, for the judging of the gaily decorated floats. Finally the last mile home, the old tram swaying and jolting through the suburbs down the steep hill to the terminus, brakes protesting at coming to a standstill, the driver pulling back the sliding door with a crash to walk through to the other platform for his return journey.

Down the quiet road to home, where before the war we would parade up and down on long summer Sunday evenings, sporting our best suits, to spend our hard-earned coppers on the giggling girls in the soft-drinks bar near the village. The next day I took a train out into Derbyshire, to walk the lanes and paths of the quiet countryside, where the remoteness and beauty of my surroundings made such a rewarding contrast from the steel city but a few short miles away.

Here again I found the peace that quietened my troubled mind, looking down at last on a tiny village as the evening mists, rolling down from the hills, finally obscured it from view, with only the church steeple visible for a moment until it too succumbed.

I left home, somehow glad to be going back, to return and face whatever there was to come, no longer having to suppress my fears, content in the knowledge I would once more be with 'them'.

(I noted in my log book at that time, April 1944, that since spring 1943, Bomber Command had flown 74,900 sorties, aircraft lost 2,824, aircrew killed or missing over 20,000.)

The campaign to destroy rail centres and some airfields south of the invasion beaches was by then well under way, and results were excellent, causing disruption on a tremendous scale with our losses kept to a minimum.

Raids on Hasselt, Orleans on two occasions, Tergnier and as far south as Angers were completed successfully, although the opposition was still active. On the raid to Angers, after a long approach from seaward via the west coast of France, we were proceeding northward on the run home, and I was feeling quite secure as M for Mother roared at low level above French villages, their inhabitants turning out into the streets, ignoring the blackout, the lights from open doors clearly seen.

Suddenly a twin-engined aircraft with a light in the nose appeared above us on the starboard quarter; for a minute I hopefully imagined that one of our own Mosquito aircraft, acting as an intruder, was perhaps being sociable. The illusion was shattered as it turned in for an attack. Our skipper's evasive action at that height was admirable. We turned and jinked from starboard to port, and the enemy fired a near miss as he tried to follow. A second burst from both Dougie and from me kept him at bay for a few minutes, then a determined attack, as we passed over a built-up area, brought him so close that I became hypnotised for a terrifying moment. I thought he would surely ram us, but his cannon-fire passed below, and suddenly, inexplicably, ceased altogether, long before he reached us and broke away to starboard.

My guns had also fallen silent at the end of a long burst at the fighter which had flown directly into it. Further fire from Dougie followed him into the darkness as I vainly endeavoured to clear the stoppages.

With the wireless operator and Dougie keeping a watchful eye open, I removed my leather gauntlets in an effort to get some feeling in my fingers, and to find the cause of my guns' failure, until the tips grew numb through the silk under-gloves and there was still no response when I pressed the firing buttons. In the meantime our adversary had disappeared and we pressed on towards the Channel coast. Our luck had held again, though I could hardly believe that we had escaped unscathed.

We were halfway across the Channel before I got some response to my efforts and achieved a short burst from two of the Brownings, only for them to jam again. My fingers were now so frozen that there was no feeling in them, so I replaced my leather gloves and banged my hands together to try to restore the circulation. It was some weeks later before the tips of my fingers lost their numbness.

The momentous month of June commenced with a short trip across to Calais, led by those winged legends the Mosquitoes using Oboe, an infallible method of marking with remarkable accuracy, the aircraft flying along a beam at a given speed and height until the signal for bomb release was given by a cross beam. We would release our bombs when the Mosquitoes dropped theirs, and the results were extremely accurate.

The skipper, navigator and bomb aimer, were now commissioned, while Dougie, Tobin and I had been promoted to flight sergeants, and our proficiency as blind markers gave us some status as a senior crew.

Briefing was unusually late on 4th June, and the station was confined to camp. It was early evening when we assembled before the huge wall map. Although no mention of the landings in Normandy were made, the fact that our operational height was way below normal, with coastal batteries as the target, left no doubt that the Big Show was on. As Primary Blind Markers, our timing and approach had to be spot-on.

As we crossed the Channel, Geoff's remarks about the number of blips on his H2S radar tube convinced us that the mighty Armada was on its way. I longed to get a sight of this great concentration of ships of every description, but cloud hid them from view. After a careful run-up at six thousand feet, we turned for a short trip home without incident, and my thoughts were with the lads below, who would be taking the brunt of the opposition to the first landings.

Frequent trips to marshalling yards, and a further four operations to flying bomb sites and their supply depots, kept the Group busy for the next few weeks. Again Mosquitoes using Oboe, and Lancasters fitted with the same device, ensured accurate marking. Some flak claimed one or two aircraft, but we remained unscathed.

Air superiority was marked by daylight operations to Oisemont and Rollez, the supply points for the VI sites, which were hammered unmercifully. The novelty of entering enemy territory in broad daylight escorted by hordes of fighters was indicative of the air mastery achieved. Returning across the Channel, I could clearly observe the warships off the French coast, firing their broadsides in support of the British and American Forces, and the wake of hundreds of vessels, arrowing their way backwards and forwards, almost bridging the narrow stretch of water.

Our last daylight operation for a while entailed a ground support raid by over one thousand bombers to Cagny near Caen on the eighteenth of July. Montgomery's armies had been held for some time by the spirited resistance of the German forces massed in the area; despite heavy losses by both sides, stalemate had ensued.

The spectacle that morning was unforgettable. Perhaps our troops below were heartened as they watched the never-ending bomber stream approach, heard the echoing thunder of thousands of engines blanked out by the mass of high explosive which caused the area around the ill-fated town to erupt and suffer obliteration. Columns of smoke towered up as load after load of bombs cascaded in the highly concentrated attack. The German forces must have been stunned and bewildered at this display of Allied air power, yet even after this, the greatest ground support operation ever undertaken, they resumed their stubborn defence within a few days, and it took all the heroism and determination of our soldiers finally to overcome the unbelievable tenacity of the defenders.

From my position high above the battlefield I watched, overcome by the sheer spectacle of the number of aircraft involved, staring silently below at the earth being ripped and torn apart. As we banked steeply away, the cloud of smoke and dust was increasing to enormous proportions, highlighted at the base by the flash of explosions as the hordes of aircraft released their loads.

A Lancaster passed to my right, spiralling down and down, leaving a curving trail of smoke. Another flew on and on in flames, the crew baling out, their descent appearing never to end until lost to view against the background of the earth so far below. Losses that day were reported as negligible in proportion to the aircraft involved, but there were some who made the supreme sacrifice, perhaps after surviving many raids over Germany with all that entailed. They were in my thoughts as we crossed the coast of England, once again to leave it all behind.

In the late evening of that day we returned to attack Wesseling, and to receive some damage from heavy flak over the target-a sharp reminder, if one was needed, that the opposition had still to be reckoned with.

Two days later we flew a diversionary sortie, one of a hundred aircraft, to the oil storage depot at Donges near St Nazaire, while the main attack that night was on Kiel with a further diversion by Mosquitoes on Berlin. Few aircraft were lost, and the German controllers were completely deceived by the sophisticated planning.

The resumption of operations over the prime target Germany began the following night, and any ideas that the enemy's fighter defences had diminished were soon to be dispelled.

CHAPTER NINE

Back to Germany

As I took my place in the turret before the engines were started, the sweat began to form on my forehead, trickling down from underneath my helmet in the warm evening air.

M for Mother lifted ponderously to begin the slow climb to operational height, and I tried to recall our experiences on previous ops to Stuttgart, our target for the night.

My mind was easier than for some time past. The mental battle had been won, and in its place a sense of resignation was backed by a glimmer of hope. It was of little use to live in constant fear of what might happen, and the proficiency of the crew allowed a hope for ultimate survival, despite the probability of violent death. And the immediate emergencies of combat left no room in the mind for philosophy, only an automatic reaction that brought to the fore all the skills learned in training and (more important) the later experience.

Now in the intervals between operations I no longer anticipated an end, and enjoyed to the full the nights out and the other activities that were enhanced by the supreme comradeship of the times. The shadow of the suppressed dead-weight of feeling for the loss of so many good friends I never now allowed to come to the fore.

After the interlude of flying the short sorties over France, the long leg out to Stuttgart seemed interminable. The complete cloud cover decided our marking procedure, dropping sky marker-flares blindly by the H2S that had proved such a boon to our navigation.

Once again that straight and level routine on the run-up, with heavy flak coming up all around us belying any thought of invincibility I might have entertained.

As our flares were being released and the tension was becoming unbearable, two enemy fighters appeared high above. I passed on the information to the skipper, then as Dougie picked them up they overtook us and were lost to view, and his warning that they were turning back, still high overhead, left me searching frantically for them. Finally I saw them as they simultaneously dipped their wings to streak down way behind a four-engined aircraft entering the now brightly illuminated arena. Their victim dived away to the right, climbed steeply to hang almost stationary, or so it seemed, as flames began to stream back from the wings. Then a terrific explosion, here and there the sparkle of target indicators, identifying the stricken aircraft as one of our Group, and a pall of smoke slowly mushrooming, while other Lancasters nearby maintaining their steady course, one of them releasing flares.

Then we were away and flying through weird monstrous shapes of storm clouds, towering on either side, while lightning flashed and hailstones rattled against the perspex, and at last to the Channel coast. It was some time later, after de-briefing, when I was shaken to hear that Bill's crew had failed to return. Recently in the Mess I had taken the opportunity to talk to him again, but he had still been disinclined to pursue our conversation. He had always been a complex person, and at that time totally unhappy with his lot. As time went on, and no reports of his survival came to hand, the picture of that exploding Lancaster returned into my mind, and I wondered if it had held his crew. Whether it had or not, they had just disappeared, like too many before them.

The following evening saw us outward-bound again for Stuttgart, leading the attack as Primary Blind Markers, in weather that was atrocious. Electrical storms brought the hazards of severe icing, and our aircraft was buffeted like a toy. There was complete cloud-cover again over the city as our flares went down, and my eyes never left the sky above, tempting as it was to glance below. Then a farewell burst of flak alongside as we reached the darkness, the weary drag back, the weather still deteriorating until we touched down, exhausted after almost fifteen hours in the air for the two consecutive operations.

I had now completed thirty-eight trips, counting the sorties to France. The reaction amongst the crews can be imagined when some chair-borne individual introduced a points system, under which sorties other than over Germany would not be regarded as full operations. I felt that, if that was to be the case, then any op to Berlin should have counted as two.

The crew had decided to visit London on the leave which was now due. My preoccupation with operations had led to some delay in my replies to Tina's letters. Consequently relations between us had hardened somewhat. I needed little persuasion, therefore, to join the others, while feeling a little selfish in avoiding the journey to Wickenby. A riotous week it turned out to be. We returned broke but well satisfied that we had left our mark on the capital city.

It was an agreeable surprise to be briefed the next day for a raid ahead of our troops in Normandy against German concentrations of armour. This was to be repeated twenty-four hours later by a second successful attack, and I was full of satisfaction at the opportunity of supporting our soldiers. Some light flak was encountered, but we returned without undue incident.

Back to Germany, with an attack on the Opel works at Russelheim, where hazy conditions thwarted the visual markers. Reverting to Blind Backers-Up, we bombed on time, but the general opinion was that the indicators were scattered and so, therefore, was the bombing.

Four days later in the forefront of an attack on Kiel, as Bob, in that unconcerned monotone of his, was counting off the seconds to release the flares, a mighty explosion just outside the turret brought my hands up across my face in a vain gesture of protection. A large cloud of oily smoke with a flaming centre hung in the air, convincing me that the German defenders were sending up 'scarecrows', simulating an aircraft going up in flames, to put off the crews who were approaching the target area.

I had seen such devices before, and a series of them did, from a distance, look very much like aircraft being shot down. This particular one exploded almost in my lap. If it had been heavy flak, there is no doubt our aircraft would have sustained serious damage, but in the event we flew serenely onward, with only the rear gunner quaking.

In anticipation of the probability of the cloud cover which had spoiled the previous raid we were briefed as Blind Sky Markers. After a long diversionary approach our run-up to the aiming point was precise and on time, despite close encounters with heavy flak that made me recoil in the cramped space available, ducking my head after one particularly close explosion, unheroically praying that Bob would release our flares and let us get to hell out of there.

As at last we turned on the first leg out of the target area, I noticed another Lancaster, close by on my left and slightly higher, clearly discernible in the reflected glow from the target, on the same heading as ourselves. Our aircraft must have been more clearly silhouetted to its crew, situated as we were between them and the brilliance of the night sky we had just vacated over the objective.

Unconcerned, I rotated away to my right, to search the area below and towards the receding target, in time to see a Focke-Wolfe 190 approaching. I had just prepared the skipper for the appropriate evasive action, to be precipitated on the command 'Go', when the perspex of my turret, on my left and just above my head, disintegrated all around me, bullets ricocheting from the guns and mountings, the reflector sight a few inches in front of my face twisting at a crazy angle.

A sharp intake of breath as I croaked 'Go-go!' and the wad of gum in my mouth stuck in my throat as I pressed my back hard against the doors to avoid the hail of fire. A faint voice in my ears as one of the crew remarked, 'Poor old Smithy', mistaking my choking for mortal wounds.

The sound of Dougie's guns firing and we were going down and down, the stream of bullets leading out and away from me, a glimpse of the enemy cannon fire streaming across obliquely. Dougie continued the running commentary as I hung on fearfully, our aircraft twisting and turning violently until eventually we flew on, weaving from side to side.

A chance to take stock of the situation, pieces of perspex hanging loose, moving inward with the pressure from the slipstream, my right knee suddenly painful as I stood up to look below, warm blood trickling down my leg. Everyone talking at once until quietened by the skipper. Some nervous amusement when I cleared my throat and explained the reason for my choking, my knee only gashed just below the kneecap when I jerked backward and caught it on the gun mountings.

There was no doubt we had been fired on by the Lancaster, the most likely explanation being that one of the gunners having also seen the enemy fighter approaching had decided to 'have a go'.

Well out over the sea I lit my cigarette, a full sense of elation flooding through me as I examined, with interest, the series of jagged holes on my left, with the two panels almost completely shot away up top.

On the skipper's instructions I left the turret, squeezing Dougie's leg as I passed his position on my way up front, a smile at Tobin, in his tiny compartment surrounded by equipment, and at Geoff, hunched over his navigator's table, finally to stand beside the skipper, the unaccustomed heating warm and pleasant after the Spartan discomfort of the position I had vacated.

The following day, our Gunnery Leader queried Dougie having returned the fire from the offending Lancaster. As we were leaving the section, we met the skipper who, upon hearing our comments, went to see the Gunnery Leader, returning grim-faced after informing him that we were under our captain's command, and that he approved of Dougie's reactions. Some opinions suggested that the Lancaster could have been controlled by the enemy, but were hardly credible. Most important was that we had survived again. How long could our luck hold out?

Even after the seven hour trip to Russelheim and the aftermath of the tense encounter that had so nearly been my end, exhausted as I was, sleep evaded me. The snores of my friends from upstairs, as well as Bob's efforts just across the room we shared, brought a smile of affection to my face. Slipping on my battle-dress, I let myself out of the back door that opened out on to the grass verge overlooking the airfield, to climb over the wire fence and on to the perimeter track that passed close to the semi-detached married quarters we used as billets.

It was just after dawn, when the sun had not quite made it up to the tree-fringed horizon, and a summer morning, so specially typical of this island of ours, which brought memories flooding back of other early mornings, camping out in the clearings of the extensive woodlands that surrounded my home, where my friends and I roamed free, to become an Errol Flynn or Douglas Fairbanks, driving off the enemy in many a pitched battle. Or in our hides, to watch the unwary rabbit, or even, on occasions, a crafty fox, standing for a moment, head uplifted, never quite sure that all was well.

I walked as far as the first dispersal, to lean against the tyre of a recumbent Lancaster and light a second cigarette, only to throw it down and grind it into the oil-stained concrete, the taste unpalatable and bitter on my tongue. The station was already awakening, and a small truck passed abreast of the aircraft hangars, to speed off along the far side of the perimeter and stop near the control tower.

The sun lifting over the trees was now working on the lengths of mist that still enshrouded the aircraft waiting in their distant dispersal's, waiting for their ground crews who would bring them to life, the riggers, mechanics and electricians, the armourers, who handled the multiple bomb loads with practised ease, whose comrades had died in a recent tragedy when unloading bombs from an aircraft that had returned from a cloud-covered French target. The load exploded, killing several men outright and terribly injuring others. Four of the bodies were never traced. Now the enormous crater was filled, and the business of war continued. No time to remember, no public acclaim.

Another cigarette, and the wire fence caught my hand, the spike embedded deep below my thumb. Upstairs the snores quietened to deeper sleep, water cold on my hand. I settled to sleep more content now, no I was not afraid any more. How often did I try to convince myself? Then Geoff was pulling back the bed covers and ignoring my protests, when all I wanted was to huddle down and let my mind drift away on pleasant things, as we all do when a warm bed seems like heaven on earth when you know you have to leave it.

To learn at breakfast that ops are on again; a cool letter from Tina, another from home. My brother is missing in the Middle East. Kiel again, using the Blind Sky-Marker technique, a shorter trip only four hours or so, no deep penetration like the long grind to Berlin, so the conversation goes on while I think, 'My brother is missing.'

Across the North Sea, thoughts of him lost are in the background of my mind, as flak rises from the coast ahead. The run-up, precise. An easy target to find on H2S. Bomb doors closed, we bank away, the Lancaster above us under careful observation, as we remember the episode of the night before.

A twin-engined fighter, tiny in the distance, his wings reflecting the glow from the holocaust below, approaches in a wide arc. The skipper curtly acknowledges my warning and I turn the turret on the beam as far as it will go. Still the enemy tightens his turn, to arrow in ahead, out of my range. Dougie fires a long, long burst, and screams, 'I've got him, I've got him!' Down to port. My body is held against the side of the turret as we straighten up to see the enemy dive away, with smoke pouring from his starboard engine.

Later, when I told the Gunnery Leader that I hadn't fired a shot, he could not, or would not understand why. My final remarks were insubordinate and vicious, and I walked disconsolately to the Mess, still angry at someone who knew it all although he had not been there.

Three days of training made a welcome break. We flew exercises that enabled Geoff and Bob to perfect their techniques in the use of H2S and other radar aids.

In fighter practice we dived and corkscrewed across the summer skies, and later, with pride and satisfaction, heard the bewildered fighter pilot mutter, 'Do you always go bloody mad like that?'

I wrote long letters to the War Office, appealing for more information about my brother, and others to mother, trying to console her and allay her fears for me.

Drinking too much, uncaring now, living for the moment there and then, to crawl between the sheets and sleep as only the drunk can.

The last day of the month, the tannoy calling, 'All air crew to the Briefing Room.' Tapes across the map, this time encompassing nearly nine hours. Over the North Sea, across Denmark, and the Baltic to the turning point, over neutral Sweden, to approach the northern coast of Germany and our distant objective, Stettin.

Our return journey would be south of Berlin, and the leg home over France. We left the English coast low over the sea, white breakers crusting the outline, the sun suffusing the light cloud with gold. Still enough daylight to see other Lancasters on either side, the familiar outlines showing the grace and power of these wonderful aircraft.

I turn the heating up slightly and settle down comfortably. A long night lies ahead and I take advantage of the trouble-free first leg, before we climb to cross the Danish coast. No fearful anticipation any more, on this my forty-sixth operation. Thoughts turn to home and my mother, still anxiously awaiting news of my brother, and to Tina, whose letters are becoming more infrequent, and I can't bring myself to care, as I had in the far off days at Wickenby.

Somehow I knew that the fear would return when the flak came near, over the target or searching the blackness in the heart of Germany. There is a change in the uniform whine of the four Merlins as we commence the climb, dark now, still with the long, low line of daylight on the horizon, ever narrowing until it disappears. Flak comes up as we cross into Denmark, but it is well below us. I wonder if the fighters will turn up: they must by now be plotting our course and trying to estimate our destination as we appear on their radar.

Nothing to be seen over the Baltic until the change of course, and then way down on my left I see a city's lights that twinkle through the blackness like a diamante brooch. I wonder how life is down there in neutral Sweden.

The target just ahead, the Lancaster skidding left, a slight adjustment right, bomb-doors open, and suddenly we are enveloped in intense bluish light as a searchlight fastens directly on us, to be followed by others, until every detail of the turret is revealed. I try to shade my eyes to no avail, the glare is constant, unmoving.

Our run-up continues, flak now all around, the multiple explosions causing the aircraft to shake and shudder. Bob's voice-'steady-steady', then the fear takes over, coming up from my stomach, knotted in the knowledge that this is it, after all.

The blinding lights are still there as we fly on, like a cat on a wall in the darkness, followed by a torch-beam – no matter how fast he runs a slight movement of the hand keeps him in focus. 'Bombs gone!' And away we dive, gradually losing the cursed lights, now sweeping down to an oblique angle, reluctant to lose the fly held in their web. The crew are silent, there is nothing before my eyes except weird reddish shapes that float across my vision, resulting from the brilliance I could not avoid.

The long hours pass as our faithful aircraft roars on through the darkness above the agony of an enemy whose frontiers are assailed to East and West but are still fighting on, controlled by the maniacs who have brought misery, degradation and death to untold millions. We cross the Allied lines as dawn lightens the early morning, then the open sea is grey below, until we pass at last above the familiar landscape of England. The 'thud-thud' as the undercarriage is selected down, the fields opening up around us, to race by as the runway appears and lengthens. We touch down for a perfect landing.

The seven of us, tired beyond the urge to speak, have little to say as the crew-bus rattles at speed to de-briefing. The WAAF driver crashes the gears noisily.

The hot drink, the Intelligence Officer's patient questions, breakfast in the Mess, and the walk back to the avenue of houses where we live to lie for a while, fully clothed on our beds, in the quiet.

The sun, streaming across from the window, shafting down through the curl of the cigarette smoke.

CHAPTER TEN

Carry On

In early September 1944, the newspaper in the ante room carried banner headlines as our victorious troops entered Brussels. The Americans' progress was equally impressive, and the enemy was reeling back towards his frontiers in confusion.

We all contributed to the general opinion that it was as good as over: if the Allied Armies continued like this, they would soon be in Berlin, and true air superiority by day had been a major factor in the success of our armies. From the word 'Go' our fighters had roamed the battlefields at will, destroying anything that moved behind the enemy lines.

Our experiences in the previous months, however, clearly showed that at night the German defences were still as active as ever. They might have been scraping the barrel as far as aircraft were concerned but they were still a force to be reckoned with, and their pilots were almost fanatical. There was still a long way to go – it was far from over yet.

September the sixth, and ops were on after over a week's respite, during which we were still undergoing training each day, but able to spend evenings in town and catch up on much-needed undisturbed sleep at night. The target was Emden – our first venture into Germany in broad daylight. Despite the assurance of plentiful fighter support, that naked feeling persisted as we approached the enemy coast. I could not even see our escort until a flash of sunlight reflected from their wings revealed them, several squadrons, tiny specks, so high above that they seemed to be too far away if we were suddenly attacked – I would have much preferred to see them close by. I took comfort from the thought that they knew what they were doing, but that didn't prevent me from thoroughly searching the surrounding sky.

There was no sign of opposition until we were above the

estuary. Then flak came up, and puffs of smoke from the explosions raced b y astern. We turned in over the target, which stood out clearly far below. It was a bomb aimer's dream, resulting in one of the most successful raids ever. Crossing the nearby coast on the way out, we passed a Lancaster with a faint trail of smoke trailing astern, gradually losing height. After watching him for some time, I noticed two of our fighters appear from nowhere to fly alongside the ailing- bomber, until the trio were lost from view as we made our way across the expanse of the North Sea.

Another few days of training, and we were en route for a daylight attack on Gelsenkirchen in the Ruhr: the last place on earth to go to in daylight. Patchy cloud did not hinder the attack, but the flak was the worst encountered for some time. The gunners below, who must have gained much experience from the constant attentions of Bomber Command, put up a near impenetrable barrier. Preoccupied as I was with our own predicament, the sight of our comrades, flying on and on through the mass of multiple explosions, playing Russian roulette with a vengeance, filled me with awe and admiration.

It amazed me that any mind could stand the strain, could persuade the physical body to operate the controls of those aircraft with their vulnerable loads, in such surroundings; yet on they came, undeterred. Even when one exploded, with a great mushroom of smoke and flame, another appeared in its place, with a slight tipping of the wings, as if shrugging off the remnants of its predecessor, the only concession to the surrounding conflagration.

As our bombs were released, another Lancaster was engulfed in flames beneath me and, before I turned my horrified eyes away, I had a glimpse of the kaleidoscope of streets and buildings, below the falling debris, as a mighty upheaval occurred. Ringed by the percussion, the area seemed to open out for a moment, and then close up again, with minor eruptions round about: a four-thousand ponder had found its mark. I seemed to be suspended over the expanse of this predominantly built-up area until we turned away at last towards the coast. I breathed a fervent sigh of relief at the miracle of our escape.

We were down for operations on the following night, and so a binge at the local pub, to celebrate the skipper's promotion to Flight Lieutenant, and Dougie's and mine to Warrant Officer, had to wait. I spent the early part of the afternoon in scrounging a new uniform from the clutches of a reluctant Stores Warrant Officer, who was eventually persuaded of my need. The gabardine certainly looked much better than my old serge 'best-blue', but I changed hastily back into battle-dress after trying it on, and hurried back for briefing. Our destination was Frankfurt, which I remembered well from our three previous visits.

The darkness all around us as we neared the enemy coast seemed positively cosy after the daylight effort to the Ruhr the previous afternoon, but as we progressed I became conscious of a nagging pain in my stomach, and my temperature rose until the sweat began to pour off me. Even with the heating turned down I maintained the temperature, becoming faint and dizzy, with the nausea rising up to my throat and causing me constantly to swallow hard.

By this time we were nearing the target so I kept my silence. The flak was as concentrated as the day before, but looked different because of the canopy of cloud over the city.

I kept a sharp look-out above while our sky-markers were dropped and we reached the surrounding darkness. The pain in my abdomen made me gasp with agony, and suddenly there was a surge within me. I pulled away my oxygen mask in time to vomit again and again, almost blinded by the pain, while my head felt about to burst. Beginning to feel faint I replaced the oxygen-mask and breathed in its steady flow. I notified the skipper, who directed Dougie to take over my position, and Tobin to go in the mid-upper turret. I reported that I was feeling better, and continued to rotate the turret.

Gradually, the pain in my stomach and head subsided, and I thanked the Lord that we had not been attacked by any fighters. The skipper enquired every few minutes if I was OK and I was glad to reassure him.

Back at base, the Medical Of finer gave me a beaker full of castor oil-much to my disgust. Half the night was spent tearing up the stairs to the bathroom, and staggering down again feeling completely miserable. A further humiliation was that it cost me a pound note for cleaning up the turret, and no amount of protest would convince the grinning ground-crew that I had been genuinely ill. Still feeling groggy, I made my way home, thankful that our leave had become due at this time. Later on in the week, the ailment and its symptoms, which I put down to food-poisoning, finally disappeared, but try as I might I could not remember eating anything that the others had not taken.

Before I left home for my return, the postman called with a letter from the authorities, which stated that my brother was aboard a hospital ship homeward bound, suffering from dysentery and loss of memory, combined with other mental complications after his years of service in the desert. Our joy knew no bounds. Concerned as we were for his health, the fact that he was alive, after all those months of waiting, was a bonus I had dared not hope for. I left home happy at my mother's contentment.

Changing trains at Doncaster, I met our mid-upper gunner with a huge grin on his face, sporting the ribbon of the Distinguished Flying Medal, and on our return to base I found that the whole crew had been decorated, the skipper, Geoff and Bob, with the DFC, the remainder of us with the DFM.

A medium distance operation to Saarbrucken on the German-Franco border, South of Luxemburg, heralded our fiftieth sortie. The weather suggested that our role as Blind Sky Markers would be fulfilled, and we progressed above thickening cloud towards our target.

I had been standing up for some minutes, thinking how

quiet it had been so far, without a sign of any opposition, and peering below where the cloud had dispersed for a time, when I saw several pin-pricks of flashes far below. I notified the skipper instantly, and he banked abruptly to port.

Instantly, there was a series of terrific explosions off to starboard, one of which, directly below, sent us diving down and down uncontrollably. Pressed hard against the turret dome, I heard a yell and our descent continued until I was convinced that we were going down for good. I struggled to reach the release-handle in the door behind me (I now wore a pilot-type parachute, and could have vacated the turret once the doors had been slid back without having to enter the fuselage). Another voice said, 'Let the bomb load go,' bringing a sharp refusal from the skipper, and we started to pull out, the airframe creaking and vibrating under the terrific strain.

The yell I heard had come from Geoff, when a hole had appeared to his right in front of him, while pieces of shrapnel littered his navigation table. The skipper tried hard to regain our lost height but marked the target well below the normal altitude, skidding and almost side-slipping, as he determinedly followed Bob's instructions.

The journey back to base was made with the starboard inner backfiring and losing power. Receiving priority to land, our pilot made a long, careful approach. As we touched down, the aircraft spun off the runway, with the starboard undercarriage tyre in ribbons, and the rim tearing up great clods of grass, to leave a deep groove in the tortured earth.

For a moment I thought my turret-lock had become disengaged, as it was swung around in a wide arc, and we finally came to rest with the fire trucks and ambulance trundling up. After hastily evacuating the aircraft, we ran away some distance before gathering in stunned silence, looking back at the toppled giant.

We later found that the control surfaces on the starboard wing had been all but shot away, with dozens of holes in the bomb-doors, and the fuselage covered in oil from punctured hydraulics. It was obvious that we had been singularly fortunate: our luck had held again, greatly assisted by our remarkable skipper and his expertise in saving the aircraft and no doubt our lives.

For some time now we had been discussing, as a crew, the time when our operational careers should be brought to a close, as we had now almost completed two tours. Geoff, Bob, and Tobin, were convinced that the time had come.

Our imperturbable skipper, however, was determined to carry on. He also made it obvious that he would like Tony, Dougie and me to stay with him and that we should recruit a new navigator, bomb aimer and wireless operator to make up the crew.

Although his argument that we made a good team, even if we were allocated a 'sprog' navigator, sounded convincing, it would be no good wishing we had finished if our luck ran out over some future target or another.

I left the final decision for the time being, and heartily wished the question had not arisen, because the thought of the crew splitting up depressed and unsettled me. A unanimous verdict, one way or the other, would have been far preferable.

Our next trip, another daylight maximum effort, to Duisburg in the Ruhr perturbed me. The Germans were bound to be expecting us, and I well remembered the murderous barrage from our last operation in that vicinity.

It turned out almost exactly as before, with aircraft being torn apart by an almost impenetrable barrier of bursting shells, and the cold light of day made it seem more cruel to witness.

At night, I sometimes caught a fleeting glimpse of one of our own aircraft, all too often outlined after a nearby bomber burst into flames, or over the target, silhouetted against the lurid glow below. It was very different when the enemy could see where the concentration of aircraft would be and take full advantage of it, putting up a concentrated barrage that had to be flown through to reach the aiming point.

On this raid, however, they paid dearly for the casualties inflicted on our aircrew, for thousands of tons of bombs left towering clouds of smoke, still clearly visible all the way to the coast. But if anything were needed to convince my cremates that enough was enough, that operation was it. With multiple squadrons of fighters as escort, opposition from the Luftwaffe had been non-existent, but the flak was a different matter. The sheer volume of it had shaken them badly, and I could well understand their logic.

Nevertheless, we completed a further sortie the following night to Wilhelmshaven, when a near miss slightly damaged our starboard fin, missing the rudder itself; on examination at base it looked as if something had taken a huge bite out of it, the edges around the remaining structure smooth and even.

Our last operation together as a crew, was to be our old adversary Stuttgart, and most of us were superstitious enough not to take this fact lightly. On the way out cloud began to develop, as it always did around this particular objective.

The turret tilted to port as we turned for the run-in, while a fighter hurtled past in the opposite direction, unseeing, and all but colliding with our aircraft. He was gone in an instant, but the result if, at that precise moment, we had not been changing course, did not bear thinking about.

Our bomb aimer released the markers for the last time and we reached the turning point for the distant coast, despite all the efforts of the defenders far below, who put up a frightening barrage of fire. I stood up to peer below sometime later, when we had left the cloud behind, but all that met my anxious gaze was the black void beneath.

Tobin gave a terse warning that he had picked up what he thought was an enemy fighter on his 'Fishpond' equipment. ('Fishpond' was the name given to a small cathode-ray tube which was itself an extension of the H2S used by the navigator. It could pick up, in the form of blips, reflections of other aircraft in the vicinity, including other bombers.) The reflection that Tobin had seen was of an aircraft varying its approach and coming up fast astern. This set the adrenaline flowing, because we knew that the signals from 'Fishpond' could be picked up by the fighter's airborne radar, but despite a careful search as the distance between us narrowed, I could not see our tormentor.

Tobin maintained a constant flow of information as to his whereabouts on 'Fishpond' and when the range came down to six hundred yards on our port quarter I gave instructions to corkscrew. This started a battle of wits with our unseen adversary that went on and on; after every manoeuvre of ours, no matter how strenuous, he would begin another approach.

As the tension mounted, and I expected a hail of fire any second, our skipper finally lost patience. The situation was just up his street: he threw our Lancaster into a violent, steep dive, which I am certain it was never designed to withstand. Down and down in a breathtaking descent, with me hanging on desperately, and not a sound from the crew as we finally straightened up.

'Now can you see the bastard?' he asked. There was a gasp from the wireless operator and, after a time, confirmation that our pursuer had disappeared. Still trying to recover from the hair-raising aerobatics, I smiled to myself: the German must have wondered where the hell we had gone as we continued on our way, still wide-eyed, and on the alert for any resumption of his approach. Nothing more was to be seen of him as we left the continent astern, and the experience was a fitting finale for our three friends, who would no longer make up the team that had been so closely-knit, and with a mutual trust so dearly earned, in the preceding years.

What a party we had that nights We were joined by another crew who had completed their second tour, and I shall never forget their faces, flushed with elation that for them it was all over.

My own decision had been made: I had no wish to be posted as an instructor to Training Command, admirable though that Command may have been. I was to meet aircrew from these units later, and witnessed their frustration at being denied the opportunity to join an operational squadron.

The charisma of squadron life, despite the risks-or because of them – was impossible to emulate elsewhere, and the decision to stay on by Dougie, Tony and me was made to the delight of our skipper. There were many times I was to regret it in the months ahead.

If numbers had been the only consideration, replacing our three crew members would have been no problem: replacements from the Pathfinder Force Training Unit nearby were becoming plentiful, and squadron losses, although too regular for peace of mind, were nothing like the grievous figures of a few short months ago. Nevertheless, within the ever-shrinking frontiers of Germany, defences were still lethal enough to make the crossing of most target areas a hazardous undertaking. There was little evidence to encourage complacency. Heavy flak took its toll in deadly concentrated barrages and, despite the undoubted supremacy of our own fighter squadrons in daylight hours, night fighters still roamed the sky to press home their attacks.

Dougie, Tony and I were therefore pleased to hear that the skipper had acquired the services of a wireless operator with as many ops to his credit as we had ourselves. Within a few days he became assimilated and was happy with us. His cheerful personality was underlined by a quiet acceptance of his role – an attitude that was so often found among the aircrew. Experience had left its mark, indelible, yet undefinable by anyone who had not shared it. In the meantime we were not available for ops until a navigator and second navigator/bomb-aimer could be allocated, and we made the most of this free period with outings to Peterborough and Huntingdon, trying to compete with the Yanks who had taken over those towns.

One morning, I was approached by the Flight Commander, who suggested that I make up another crew for operations that evening. 'Be a nice change for you, Smithy,' he grinned wickedly, 'They need a mid-upper gunner.'

Although I had, on very rare occasions, occupied this position when Dougie and I changed places during some boring cross-country exercise, it had been more for the novelty than anything else. Actually to operate over Germany in a strange turret and, much more important, with a comparatively inexperienced crew sent a shiver of genuine fear through me. As I made my way to briefing, doubts raced through my mind. 'Where's your sense of adventure now?' I asked myself. 'Serves you bloody well right for being here at all, you should have packed it in when you had the chance with the others.'

I cast sidelong glances at the fellows I would be flying with to the Ruhr (of all places). They had greeted me with some reserve, yet with respect for my experience. I nevertheless felt somewhat alien, an intruder, finding it difficult to relax, and we left the room with my speaking hardly a word.

Out at dispersal later the ice was broken a little, as we smoked a last cigarette before taking up our positions in the waiting Lancaster. In the unfamiliar surroundings on top of the fuselage, I became acutely aware of my vulnerability in comparison with the usual position in the rear turret. Up here I could see everything, looking down on the great expanse of the wings' surfaces, the propellers turning to a blur, as the four Merlins were run-up individually.

As we taxied out for take-off, my complete circle of vision was a revelation. Even so, as I looked astern, down to the top of the rear turret, I would gladly have changed places with its occupant.

I waved half-heartedly to the remnants of my own crew, who stood grinning and making rude gestures at the runway edge, and Tony's unsympathetic remarks were still fresh in my mind: 'Can I have that pair of shoes, Smithy?' and 'I'll have a pint for you down at the pub.'

The take-off was all right! And it was exhilarating, being

able to see all around, instead of taking things for granted, as I usually did, with my back to the fuselage. The voices in my ears over the intercom, though strange, seemed calm enough, and everything normal. I began to feel a little ashamed of my doubts. There was little point in worrying now, in any case. Someone reported flak ahead. I swivelled around to look, and could actually see what was coming up in front – what a novelty!

It was only a flicker in the night sky, and I wondered why he had bothered to mention it. Those doubts again? I told my inner voice to shut up. Then over the target, flak seen in more of a panorama, and I began to feel sorry for Dougie if that was what he had put up with.

A near miss, and shrapnel hit the fuselage as I ducked down. Looking ahead, I saw near to the gun muzzles a torn part of the fuselage, turned out like the lid of a tin can vibrating in the slipstream.

The pilot straightened the aircraft immediately, and the bombs were away. Ahead I could judge where the incredible mass of explosions was thinning out, and a Lancaster, breaking up just above me, seemed to do so in slow motion, all the parts staying together, drifting down in a terrible finality. Suddenly, I became aware of a small object speeding by close to my left, and reflected in the brilliant light from below. I discerned a tiny figure, writhing and kicking beneath the parachute canopy, but lost to view in an instant, below and behind. After such a prolonged absence from operations, and the strain of a day fraught with anxiety and worry about flying with a strange crew, reaction set in, and I was on edge until we reached the circuit and final touch down at base. Later, I found myself chatting freely with my companions at de-briefing, discussing something we had shared together with all that it implied. Leaving the Mess afterwards and walking slowly back to the billet alone, I was still uneasy, and even more deeply disturbed by that very uneasiness.

The next day, we were given a further leave until our

crew could be reformed. For some time, I had been feeling the need to get away on my own, to find some secluded place where perhaps a little solitude would allow me to rearrange my thoughts. Not just to collect them and file them, all neat and tidy, into little pigeon-holes, but to analyse my mind, to try to find some answers to its restlessness.

CHAPTER ELEVEN

Leave

Although, pre-war, I had always been of an adventurous nature, financial considerations had limited my horizons. Even a trip to the coast had been a rare experience. It can be imagined, then, how my frustrations grew when, after losing my boyhood freedom to roam the countryside where I had been raised, a position was found for me in a chemist's shop when my family moved to the city.

Hours were long then, over ten a day, confined within the premises, day in, day out, weeks, months, years, until the war came and I escaped. During those years of frustration, I became an avid reader, endeavouring to satisfy my thirst for the adventure that I saw no prospect of participating in myself. Fiction held little interest, but the explorations of Scott, Shackleton, or any lone explorer, would fill me with envy and an admiration which knew no bounds. Once engrossed in such a volume, I would take each step along with them, oblivious to all around me. This preoccupation, taken to excess, would bring mild reprimands from my kindly parents as I pursued my reading late into the night, often with the aid of a small torch under the bedclothes.

When completely satiated, after digesting some remarkable exploits of one of my heroes, I would turn in contrast to the poets, perusing the shelves of our public library for hours.

The descriptive powers of Gray as demonstrated in his Elegy left me enraptured. That anyone could portray his depth of feelings, with such economy of words, made me troubled and disconcerted at my own inability's.

The more I read of the classics, Wordsworth, Keats, Browning and Shelley, the greater became my certainties that here was a source of inspiration, for the betterment of the often shallow minds of mankind, so ignored by my contemporaries. In my own small way, whenever the opportunity arose, I would try to combine the two influences that were predominant in my thinking; to wander off alone, over the fields and moors which surrounded our city in such splendour, making mental notes of all that nature had to offer; or in some isolated camp site, to gaze into the night sky, always aware of the faith endowed by my religious upbringing, utterly convinced of a greater being, which, though far beyond my understanding, yet provided a solace and joyous affinity that welled within me, in appreciation of all I had seen and all that lay in glorious abundance above and around me.

On my return home, in some obscure corner, I would find paper and pencil and endeavour to record what I had witnessed. After the long indoctrination that war had brought of fear and death, and of adventure in violent form, the need to get away to find perhaps a little of the poetry of life again became paramount, and I soon found the means. With doubtful legality, I bartered a spare pair of flying boots, with the added persuasion of a few pounds, for the loan of an ancient Norton motorcycle from an armourer corporal with whom I had become acquainted. I had learned to ride during my service with the RAF Regiment, though my proficiency left much to be desired. That mild October morning, I wobbled out through the main entrance, much to the amusement of the station police near the guard room, and set off down the road.

I began to enjoy the novelty, especially of attempting long distances along the country lanes without sign of other traffic. A vague notion to visit the West Country began to form in my mind as the Norton, despite its age, ran sweetly along the quiet roads.

After a short break near Northampton, I eventually found myself in Daventry, my navigation having resulted in getting hopelessly lost. The complete absence of signposts added to the difficulties. Not that I was unduly concerned, for I was thoroughly enjoying my exploration of a part of the country that previously had been signified only by names. By this time I was handling the bike with ease and reaching speeds that I would not have dared to attempt earlier.

Passing through Banbury into Oxfordshire, I reached Burford and took great delight in walking the length of this charming village. I was tempted to stay overnight, but a friendly garage owner, having provided enough fuel to fill the tank, advised me to go on to Cirencester, and it was there that I found the ideal place to spend my few days' leave.

At first sight, all ideas of going further south left me, so overwhelmed was I by the simple serenity and beauty of the scene which appeared so unexpectedly in the early autumn evening. I had left Burford some miles behind, to begin the descent of a hill which culminated in a sharp bend at the bottom, hemmed in by tall trees.

I braked hard to an abrupt halt before reaching the long straight road that ran alongside a wide, running brook to a quaint stone bridge in the background. To my right, fronted by gardens to the road, was a row of stone cottages with the grey, speckled roofs that I had noted in Burford. Smoke was rising from tall stacks, straight up, to be sifted by the topmost branches of trees, covered in autumn tints.

On my left was a further row of terraced cottages, lowfronted, with overhanging roofs in higgledy-piggledy fashion, like an illustration from a child's fairy story, fronted by a perfect green that ran down to the running water and up to the far side of the bridge.

After hurriedly cutting the engine, as the harsh noise seemed such an affront to the breathless hush lying on the twilight air, I left the bike against a low, stone wall and walked slowly along beside the clear, sweet water that chuckled and eddied swiftly by, while rising trout splashed and played to the surface.

That there was not a soul to be seen lent further unreality to all that lay around, until I noticed the sign of an old inn retreating, as it seemed, into a little cul-de-sac. The building was almost covered in foliage, allowing only the door and windows any respite, and against the background of the trees I had mistaken it for another cottage.

I was surprised at the number of people in the bar, and conversation died as I made my enquiries for a room. The landlord's wife explained that it was off-season for them and that they had no other guests at the moment, although in the summer, even in wartime, it was difficult to cope with the number of visitors. Nods from the locals, who glanced from the good lady to myself, as our conversation proceeded, following every word.

After a few drinks, and a meal that defied rationing in all respects, I retired to my room, taking a long last look through the open window: it was quite dark now and only the sound of the hurrying stream disturbed the calm night. A comfortable bed soon brought me to the borders of sleep – borders which I crossed without resistance from an untroubled mind.

Days passed pleasantly in those ideal surroundings, walking the lanes and taking much delight in anticipating what I would find around the next corner.

One fine morning, I entered a pathless wood, penetrating to the very centre, and there found hidden flowers, that had bloomed with hardly any sunlight filtering through the closely interwoven branches of the trees above. Birds approached unafraid, as I sat on a fallen trunk in the tiny clearing, to share crumbs from my picnic.

There was a multitude of unseen life in this remote spot well aware of my presence, yet knowing instinctively, I am sure, whether I was friend or foe.

All these things, by their simplicity, and in the matchless wonder of nature, quietened and fortified my mind. Added to this was the delight of staying in the picturesque hamlet itself, which, with my comfortable accommodation, made a recipe for peace.

If love of adventure had always been a dominant factor in my make-up, I had found it to excess in war, and even learned to cope with that excess. But here, over-satiated, I had turned to solitude, to nature and the elements, and found the contrast equally satisfying.

On the evening before leaving to return to the squadron, I sat again before my open window, long after the convivial company had left the bar below for their homes, and gazed at the stars above, whose light was sufficient only to outline the tops of the trees across the green, shadowy but discernible. The slight breeze was getting stronger now, disturbing their topmost branches, adding to the sound of rushing water, shallow over the stones in the brook.

No, I was not afraid to return; I was even looking forward to the adventure and the risks involved. That I shivered involuntarily I put down to the chill of the night air.

I returned the motorcycle to its visibly relieved owner, whom, I suspected, had not envisaged seeing me, or his beloved machine, in one piece again.

In the Mess, two sergeants introduced themselves as the crew replacements, having already met the skipper earlier in the day. It appeared that their crew had been awaiting 2 posting to a Pathfinder Squadron, after completing the course at Warboys. Previously, they had flown several operations with main force, but now their own skipper was in hospital with a stomach ailment, and consequently their crew had been split up piecemeal.

I could well understand their apprehension. To lose one's crew was a major calamity, and they were obviously very anxious about the whole set-up, especially about joining us on future operations. I tried to answer all their questions, assuring them that they could not be flying with a better pilot. Keen as they were to do well, I nevertheless became uneasy as their lack of experience was revealed, and wondered what our future role would be. I was soon to find out.

For the next two weeks, we flew on training exercises,

mainly navigational and practice bombing, with only the odd fighter affiliation to give Dougie and me a break from the monotony. The Spitfire made brilliant mock attacks, coming in so close that I could clearly see its pilot grinning broadly. He didn't have it all his way, and freely admitted afterwards how impressed he had been at the skipper's evasive action. Our new crew, wondering at our pilot's skill, were equally impressed.

It was late November before we were listed for operations, and it was with mixed feelings that I took my place with the crew at briefing: my sense of adventure made the prospect intriguing, but the absence of our original navigator, bomb aimer and wireless operator disturbed me.

Our target was Essen, at the north end of the Ruhr. Two squadron aircraft had failed to return in the preceding week from a similar raid, so it seemed that the enemy defences were still active and efficient. Take-off time was unusually late at 3.05 am.

As we chatted and smoked a final cigarette at dispersal, the November night was damp, cold and pitch-dark. The glowing tips of our cigarettes were pin-points in blackness: nothing else was visible. The huge airfield was silent, brooding, awaiting the first engine's start that would be repeated around the circle of perimeter track as each aircraft followed suit. Finally, they would trundle from their dispersal's, to join the queue towards the runway, the lights of which reached across into a distance that appeared to have no ending, but was all too short, with a full bomb load, and petrol tanks filled to capacity.

I could feel the tail-end lift as our Lancaster, reluctantly at first, surged ahead, the intervals between the runway lights shortening as they flashed by and receded behind me. I gave a quick thought for Dougie, high up in the fuselage, and felt the heart-warming assurance that my own pilot was at the controls. The undercarriage thudding up into its housing, and we are on our way, taking our chance with several hundred others.

Who could foretell what the next few hours would bring? Perhaps an unlucky hit, from the concentrated flak we were bound to meet, that would end it all quickly. Or severe damage, that would mean we bailed out if we were lucky, to descend into what? Or a blast from an enemy fighter, that would mean the ground-crew cleaning out the turret with a hose, after the remains had been removed on our return False heroics? Exaggeration? These things happened, and had best be said.

On this night, before we even reached the enemy coast, I could sense that our new navigator was unsure of himself. A voice in your ears at times like this can reveal so much. Hesitancy, fear, until you restrain yourself from crying out, 'Speak up for God's sake, be sure of what you are saying,' as the skipper asks three times for the change of course.

We carry a normal bomb load, mostly HE, no incendiaries. After the pasting Essen has received, what is there left to burn? We have reverted to 'supporters' on this trip, but we must endeavour to reach the target on time, to make up the numbers, to join the Pathfinders carrying markers. Some 'supporters' we are, I think when our navigator cannot even find the bloody Ruhr!

Suddenly a wave of compassion for the poor sod, trying his best no doubt, and scared out of his wits. Perhaps he cannot think rationally, and that has happened to us all. These thoughts conflicted in my mind. At that moment, I too was greatly afraid, and how I wished to God I had not decided to go on. Previously, when I had been obliged to accept the fact that a certain number of ops had to be completed, I had done so, although often in fear. But to have had the opportunity to finish, and still to go on-that was different!

Now, I had begun to feel resentful of the slightest obstacle, real or imaginary, that might come between me and survival. The run-in seemed never ending. I answered the skipper's enquiry 'OK Smith?' curtly and clearly, trying to encourage our navigator that all was well.

As often in the past, the blackness erupted in a crescendo

of noise and flames, while predicted flak bracketed our shuddering aircraft. The skipper's instant reaction sent the Lancaster down and down into a stomach-churning dive, forcing me against the turret structure, unable to move. The multiple explosions everywhere, no gaps, no space, only the sharp metallic crack of bursting shells and the rattle of shrapnel along the fuselage.

No respite, the skipper cursing obscenely as, no matter which way we turned or dived or climbed, the explosions followed. At last a break, and his voice urging the navigator to re-check his calculations. The second navigator muttering unintelligibly, as he endeavours to help to fix our position. Far to my right, I see flares strung across the blackness, then markers streaming down. Dougie spells it out, before I could switch on my intercom, that we are well south of our objective. I feel the pressure as we turn hard to starboard.

Running up to the target, hopelessly late, on full power, and again we enter a murderous barrage over Essen. Our bombs fall away and glancing down, I can see the indicators glowing deep red far below, only to be obscured at intervals by patches of cloud, that thicken to a continuous cover, as the mass of explosive reaches the ground and churns up the remains of the tortured city.

A course for our return to the coast, after a number of amendments by our now demoralised navigator, who apologises for every alteration. The English countryside awakening below, a sudden ocean of mist that hides everything but the tops of hills like islands. Then clear again, a panorama of fields and hedgerows, that gradually take on individuality as we descend towards the airfield. I light another cigarette from the butt of the last one, shove the crumpled packet into the knee-pocket of my flying suit. Permission to land, undercarriage down, turret locked astern, the fields open up around me and we are bumping along the runway, to turn off to dispersal.

Engines off, I sit for a brief moment, my helmet pushed

back from my forehead. My watch says 7.30: we have been airborne only four and a half hours and I cannot believe it. After de-briefing, and breakfast, the room in the billet is ice-cold. I try to sleep. I can see the flak bursting all around. I sweat, and the room is so cold.

Less than thirty-six hours later, we took off early for the Ruhr again, our objective Duisburg, to attack the enemy's vital remaining oil stocks, of which a third were said to be situated in the area. How I hated the very sound of that name, the Ruhr: the whole complex was a death trap, and its defences never seemed to diminish. Some targets, such as isolated cities, you could call a 'piece of cake', but the Ruhr always provided a murderous barrage that seemed impossible to fly through.

This visit was to be no exception. After again arriving late, we crossed the target in a hail of fire, a Lancaster nearby exploding in an enormous pall of black smoke, pieces from the stricken aircraft spiralling out from the centre, and our own aircraft tossed aside by the tremendous explosion. Long after we had left the area, I could see the pulsating glow from the fires, and the clouds of smoke reflecting the inferno below.

Back at dispersal, a large hole at the edge of the entrance door in the rear of the fuselage was discovered. Although nothing vital had been hit, I tried to evaluate the odds and the results of that lump of shrapnel hitting my turret. When I voiced my fears, as one does after such an escape, the remarks of the crew left me in no doubt: I could never have become a father.

The weather in the early days of that December, 1944, effectively grounded the squadron. When it finally cleared, out we went on air exercises for the benefit of our navigators.

The second week, and we reported to briefing for operations. When the target was uncovered, we could hardly believe it was the Ruhr once again. Essen! Memories of the raid a fortnight previously haunted me, and I fervently hoped our navigators would get it right this time.

It was not to be. A disastrous error was made, and we arrived over the target long after the attack had got under way. The skipper's voice indicated his annoyance and, after passing through the tremendous network of the massed antiaircraft fire, a strained silence imposed itself during the run for home. After consulting the Squadron Navigation Leader next day, the skipper informed us that both of our replacements had been posted.

Although their time with us had been short-lived, I half regretted their departure, for we had come to know each other well. On several occasions, in the more relaxed atmosphere of the village pub, they had confided in me their misgivings as to their respective abilities. I had imagined that they would improve, given time. But sentiment could not be considered: the skipper had lost patience. Superbly efficient himself, he never would accept second-best for long from anyone.

In any case, his talents were well-recognised, and I believed that the matter would have been taken out of his hands sooner or later, for our record as precision markers had been first rate. To reassume our previous seniority, we required sound and experienced navigators, and a stroke of fortune provided them to an outstanding degree.

A top Master Bomber of renowned ability had been promoted to Squadron Commander, and his navigators, both officers, were crewed with us. We again took up our role as primary markers.

Three days later, we were off on the long haul to Ulm, far down in southern Germany. Before we took our places in the aircraft, alternate sleet and hail had swept across the airfield. We fully expected the operation to be scrubbed, and awaited the signal Very light from control, but there was no such luck. We climbed laboriously up through the murk, to set course on the first leg out. The skipper's voice sounded cheerful as he checked I was OK. I had noted particularly how elated he had been at briefing, relishing the fact that we were again leading the attack as primary blind markers, in the way that was so typical of his character. I, too, was reassured that our crew was whole again. The pride in our role was infectious: what enemy, I asked myself, could forestall such a crew as this?

The navigation was masterly. We approached on time, bomb-doors gaping open, the flak sporadic as our markers were released. I looked down to see a twin-engined fighter slide across below us. The brief glimpse identified a Dornier 217 with upward-firing guns, a type I had not seen before, but as several gunners had reported its presence on a number of occasions we had studied the silhouettes carefully in the gunnery section.

I called for an immediate diving turn to starboard, and the skipper really excelled himself. I gasped as our Lancaster dropped like a stone, even before I had finished speaking, and, pressing hard against the perspex, I saw the Dornier appear to rise up past us as if on elastic. A long burst went hopelessly wide, as I struggled to remain upright, and the enemy banked hard over, to dive away back across the now brightly-lit target area.

We straightened up only to dive again without warning, which took me completely by surprise, for I had informed the skipper that the fighter had dived away, and had given no further instruction for evasive action. The sheer violence of this further manoeuvre lifted me, utterly helpless, to the turret's curved top. A fleeting glimpse of another Lancaster, horribly close, hurtling by with flames streaming from the port wing, unnerved me, and I stared transfixed, soundlessly mouthing, 'Oh my God, my God.'

The doomed aircraft carried on down and down until it entered the cloud thousands of feet below. There was a brief glow and it was gone. The skipper's voice sounded in my ears, 'OK Smith?' And again, more insistently, until I croaked a reply. All the way home that night, in appalling weather which offered some respite, that ghastly spectacle was mirrored before me. Our aircraft was thrown about in the turbulence until we crossed the English coast, but the discomfort was only a background to the horror still before my eyes.

On our return, exhausted after being airborne for almost seven hours, I fell asleep instantly, but awoke some hours later to find myself standing in the room in the pitch dark. I staggered about, my mind bemused and uncomprehending, arms outstretched, until I found my bed. I awoke late and, recalling my predicament in the night as though it were a part-remembered dream, wondered why I had found the destruction of that Lancaster so nerve-shattering. After all, I had witnessed many such scenes before.

I began to see a real meaning in the RAF slang term, 'Round the Bend'.

During late December, the weather worsened and yet again, the German High Command had a rude surprise in store for the Allies.

Although the general opinion was that our enemy was as good as finished, we were well aware, from the spirited defence on recent operations, that although his defeat was only a matter of time, he was far from making the unconditional surrender which was eventually to be imposed by our leaders. The newspaper headlines of Field Marshal Von Runstedt's offensive in the Ardennes, and its initial success, brought home the lesson, although it was hard to believe that he had such resources of armour and equipment.

Raids on Duisburg and Cologne still left us grounded, although a few aircraft from our Group flew on Army Support missions. At last the weather above the battlefields cleared. Hitler's hopes of one last major breakthrough had faded and died out in the snow and ice. Air support from the Luftwaffe was soon non-existent. Our own squadrons, which had waited so impatiently, took their toll of the retreating enemy, who turned and wearily abandoned transport and armour, the petrol tanks run dry.

That Christmas of 1944 was celebrated in no uncertain manner for it had been a momentous twelve months for the squadron. I left my comrades lingering in the Mess in the early hours of Boxing Day, after the beer had flowed unceasingly. Well 'under the weather', I stood for a moment in the icy cold. A chorus of voices, in a harmony that would have done credit to a Welsh male voice choir, pervaded the air. The fine tenor voice rose above the rest, and the words came clearly: 'Gentleman songsters all are we, doomed from here to eternity...'

Sentimental as always, the effect upon me was indescribable. Thoughts of home and Christmas past again filled my mind, with a pang of remorse that I had failed to write home regularly. My family, like millions of others, had been disrupted by war, and the close-knit unity had gone, perhaps never to be replaced.

Before I slept, thoughts of Tina came fleetingly to mind, and of the long meaningful letter in which she had left the door wide open for a reconciliation. My answer, posted just before our last operation, had been hurried, brief and noncommittal. I had closed my mind to any outside influence. I had become inward-looking, oblivious to normality and irritated by it. What had seemed important before, I now dismissed as trivial. All of this remained beneath the surface, while I drank and laughed with the others as if unconcerned. I did not ask their thoughts, nor they mine, beneath the veneer of 'couldn't care less'. I only knew that it was good to be one of them, and that they understood.

In January 1945, the weather lifted enough for the squadron to take off one late afternoon for Nuremberg. The emphasis was on the marshalling yards, and on preventing the enemy from moving supplies and reinforcements to his now failing armies along the Western Front.

After battling through dense masses of cloud, with ice building up on all wing surfaces, unable to deviate or climb above the weather, our navigators marked the target accurately and on time. I had never seen an objective obliterated by so much cloud. The field of vision was confined to our immediate vicinity; how the main force coming up behind were to locate our markers was a mystery. This was not just a case of cloud below, for all around towered huge columns, lit for brief moments by the flash of exploding shells, themselves seemingly muffled and diffused in the thick haze. On our return all the crews agreed that the weather, not the enemy, had been our main adversary.

No fighter could have achieved anything in such conditions, and Dougie and I could do little but sweat it out for the seven hour ordeal, relying on the skipper and the navigators.

Two more sorties followed that first week of the New Year to Royan and Hanover, both in similar conditions, and then we were briefed for a major attack on Munich, our fourth operation within five days. If the weather had been regarded as 'dicey' on the last series of trips, this particular night was the daddy of them all. From take-off to the target our aircraft was tossed about like a leaf. Over the continent I had settled down as patiently as possible, sealed in my tiny capsule, while the aircraft shuddered, and rose and fell. With an occasional violent thud, as if striking something solid, our Lancaster ploughed through the seemingly impenetrable barrier of icy cloud. I sat relaxed, the heated inner suit insulating my tired body from the dreadful cold of the outside temperature 30° below.

All that lay between me and the grey swirling mass of that 'outside' was the thin perspex of my cramped compartment. This was opaque now from thousands of tiny droplets of moisture compressed by the solid slipstream, except where the perspex had been cut away, immediately in front of me. Through that gap I stared at the dirty white grey mist racing astern, emphasising our speed and making me wonder how many long hours it would take to reach the target.

Turning up the heat a little I rubbed my gloved hands on my aching eyes – the lids heavy with sleep after the marathon of the previous week's flying. I contemplated the scene around me, the magazines of ammunition coming up from below, fed in metal channels from containers way back on either side of the fuselage behind me. I had adjusted the reflector sight earlier, now I checked it again, turning the control knob until the sight glowed clearly without too much brightness. With everything in order, I shifted on the parachute I sat on, and thought about my weight on the pack. Would I so distort it that the bloody thing wouldn't open if I had to bail out? No, it would be OK. I had seen the precise and careful way the WAAFs folded the things in the parachute section and dismissed the idea.

But what an alternative – to bail out and leave this comparative haven, or to stay with the aircraft! I stood up and sat down again, heavily. How solid it was beneath me! No, I would rather stay. Yet, what if I had to jump? Nearly four miles down? Still, we were over France. My thoughts turned to the reports of aircrew being lynched by outraged German citizens after bailing out, and I reached down to feel the hard outline of the Service revolver issued for such events. Defend myself and the last bullet for me. I decided it couldn't happen to me and slipped a piece of gum beneath my oxygen mask. The fresh, minty taste refreshed my mouth, and the resultant flow of saliva eased my parched throat. Suddenly we left the cloud behind, flying smoothly and already weaving gently from side to side, as the skipper automatically resumed his precautions against sudden unseen attack.

I became immediately alert and traversed the turret from port to starboard, eyes no longer heavy from fatigue but staring out into the blackness, searching, ever searching.

The intercom crackles into life, as our navigator gives the change of course to port, clearly now and confident. The run-up to Munich begins, I wonder about the population of the doomed city, with the sirens wailing, about people taking to the shelters, their thoughts, their fears and hatred. Overcast again, patchy, then the solid mass of grey, the turret perspex misting over.

The approach over the city and a gap into a weird canyon with towering cliffs of cloud on either side of us, the bomb-aimer announcing bomb doors open, steady, left, left, steady, r-i-g-h-t. Bombs away, the roar of the four Merlins now turning into a high rhythmic whine; flak piercing the gloom and rising up gracefully, to explode viciously all around the fleeing aircraft, a glimpse of another Lancaster below, a welcome sight after a nightmare of nothing for long hours, a friend. I feel almost exultant.

A tiny silhouette above hurtling down out of the overcast -a twin-engined fighter. Christ, how did he get here? I can't recognise it, turning at such an impossible angle and speeding towards us. Down we go, and Dougie fires a long burst, and I follow as the enemy passes close at incredible speed, turning again in a wide arc. Then the cloud envelops me and there's nothing but the blind crump of explosions below, a brief glitter of something far down as we cross another gap before finding again the grey anonymity.

After a period of time that never seems to end, the French coast appears, and I shift for the hundredth time to ease my aching limbs. The call to base, the WAAF's voice, clear and feminine, giving instructions to orbit the airfield. The perimeter lights in a circle below, the touch-down, and the runway, wet and shining behind me. Debriefing, the room crowded already though there are still others to come. Voices are low, as if the high spirits have not had time to resurface yet, or as if the effort needed to crack a joke, or be light-hearted, is still subdued by the giving of everything to the last seven hours.

Several days were to pass before we were outward-bound, in dopey' weather, for a major attack on the synthetic oil plant at Merseburg. Over and over again at briefing the need for accurate marking was impressed upon the assembled crews.

A Master Bomber would be in attendance- firstly, to

control the marking, and secondly to ensure as far as possible that the main force coming up behind did not bomb short of the indicators. His was an unenviable job, stoogeing around the target area until he was certain that indicators and bomb-loads had been put to good use.

Our run-up commenced with the Master Bomber calmly asking for 'Wanganui' flares that would drift over the aiming point and give a clear directive to the crews behind. Without warning, the starboard outer engine backfired and lost power. I could hear the skipper and engineer providing the remedy as the remaining engines increased their revolutions. In Erie meantime, the bomb aimer was giving instructions as if nothing was happening, and I could feel our aircraft skidding left, then right, as the skipper obeyed. The all-important flares fell away on time, and in the right place.

I was watching a Lancaster up above release its load and a four thousand pounder passing close to starboard when I felt the offending engine pick up and heard the adjustment as the power was synchronised. Looking back below, the cloud was suffused by the flash of a vast explosion, smoke came up above the cloud and it looked as if a direct hit had really started the attack well. The Master Bomber's voice sounded exultant as he repeated his instructions to the crews approaching the target.

We had just commenced a turn to starboard, on course for the distant coast, when another Lancaster slid across just below. I saw the shape out of the corner of my eye, a few seconds before the turret tilted sideways, and it was gone in an instant. If any height had been lost in our turn, we would have collided. I had flinched involuntarily, without having time to warn our pilot. The buttons, which by energising warning lights in the cockpit told the pilot to dive port or starboard, remained untouched. They were there for that very purpose – for instant reaction without using the intercom. I had hesitated that brief moment as I had thought to dive would be fatal.

Sweating profusely, I wondered afterwards if the truth was that I hadn't known what to do. I had cringed away, expecting the Lancaster to hit us, and that was that. I sat with my eyes staring into the blackness, expecting a dark shape suddenly to appear from any direction, and said not a word to the others.

Over the sea, the weather clamped down. A diversion instruction came over the air to land at a fighter station, Tangmere, on the south coast, as our own airfield was shut down. The offending engine was again running roughly, picking up for a time and then losing power. I could see only the familiar grey mass as we lost height. The voice of Tangmere control gave landing instructions to another aircraft. 'Christ, that son-of-a-bitch is early,' the skipper's Canadian drawl sounded in my ears.

At last, perimeter lights below, the starboard engine behaving perfectly, the approach along the avenue of lights until touchdown, eight hours forty-five minutes since takeoff, and my sixty-fourth operation.

Curious glances at de-briefing, only another crew already sipping their tea. The Intelligence Officer carefully writing down our navigator's responses to his questions. An audience of strangers around and behind our seated crew. Such attention and admiration at de-briefing was rare, and a line-shoot here and there was surely excusable, but the skipper was as impassive as always.

It was late afternoon before we took off for the short flight to base, after our suspect engine had been checked. Our hosts, who had made us especially welcome, gathered to see us off. In the local pub that evening, the skipper's promotion to Squadron Leader was celebrated. He paid up without complaint. Dougie and I had flown with him since he was a sergeant at Operational Training Unit in the distant days at Finningley. He remained the same quiet introvert, even at such a time as this.

A massive attack on Magdeburg, in which nearly nine

hundred aircraft were to take part, came up the next day. As we approached our objective, I tried to picture the armada behind us. If the synthetic oil plants just ahead, or anything in their vicinity, survived the assault tonight, it would be a miracle.

The defences were extremely sensitive, and explosions rocked the aircraft as we flew on steadily. Searching the sky above, I saw a Lancaster, with an engine ablaze, release its bombs to fly on and on, the lengthening flames trailing behind. A single-engined fighter approached dead astern, his tracer striking directly into the stricken bomber. As the fighter broke away, an answering stream of fire from the Lancaster gunners followed, and still it flew on, until an explosion left it falling slowly on one wing only, with the two engines on that wing clearly distinguishable. No parachutes had appeared when the cloud below hid it from view.

Behind me now the whole area was brilliantly lit. Target indicators streamed down as the backers-up re-marked the aiming point. Flak laced the sky, and the ground below was covered with eruptions as the first wave of the main force released their loads. Another Lancaster, like a flaming cross, arrowed down and I turned my gaze away, sickened by the sight.

As I rotated the turret to starboard, there was a flicker of tracer at some distance in the blackness, and a stretch of flame lit up another of our aircraft, developing quickly until, like a ball of fire, it dived down and down to hit the ground below, spreading across a landscape that had been invisible until that moment. Pitch darkness again, and all this unusual fighter activity bringing memories of the past when the German pilots had a field day.

The old fears returned, as I stood to search below, while the skipper joked the aircraft constantly. Never letting up, I covered every inch of the void around end below until we were out to sea. Leaning back, unnerved and exhausted, I was more afraid than I ever remembered in the past. Ashamed of my fears, I lit a cigarette as the aircraft lost height, but derived little comfort from the nicotine, which left me light-headed and nauseated. At dispersal, I breathed deeply, the cold air cool and refreshing on my face, and was glad to feel the concrete solid beneath my feet.

CHAPTER TWELVE

There *Is* a Future!

I was taken by surprise when the skipper beckoned me out of the gunnery section on the following afternoon. 'Find Dougie, Smithy, we have to report to the CO at three o'clock. Something's happened, though I don't know what it is.'

Our Commanding Officer eyed the three of us, with what I imagined to be a grim expression on his face. After he had outlined the purpose of our presence there, I realised that what he was telling us was being said with profound regret. Our operational careers were at an end. He indicated a signal from Group before him, but the remainder of his words, his congratulations and appreciation for our service with the squadron, were lost to me beneath the impact of the decision.

I followed my friends out, and down the long corridor of the headquarters building, half-elated and half saddened by the news. The prospect that I would not be called upon again for operations, which had preoccupied my every thought for so long, simply stunned me, and my crew-mates were equally affected. No more to be looking forward, ticking off each operation, until a given number were completed. I had only that morning contemplated where our next briefing would take us. Now without warning it was all over, finished. Life suddenly crowded in around me. The barrier my mind had erected against normality crumbled and fell. No longer would I be supported by a single purpose, paying no heed to anything but the immediate future.

Later in the day, the crews were called to briefing. I hesitated, and then remembered. As the Mess emptied, I picked up a discarded newspaper, but the words didn't register. Rain spattered against the windows and, rising to my feet, I walked down the short corridor to the billiards room. Picking up a cue, I struck a red ball hard, and watched it rebound up and down the table.

The award of the DSO to our skipper was announced the next day, before he departed on leave, on posting as an instructor. We had a few drinks together. On our return to the airfield, we shook hands before separating. The warmth of his thanks for what I had done as his rear gunner embarrassed me, as I had never known him to show his feelings so openly before.

As he walked off towards the Officers' Mess, I turned and watched his tall figure before it disappeared into the gloom. He had thanked me for my part in our long and eventful association. I had replied, knowing my response to be inadequate, fully aware that without his dedication, courage and skill, none of us would have survived.

I have not had the opportunity to meet him since that night in 1945, before his subsequent return to Canada. So, I take this opportunity to say thank you, Squadron Leader Jack Cuthill, DSO, DFC. I, for one, will never forget.

Several days later, I heard that I was posted to Warboys, the Pathfinder Training Unit, a few miles distant. In what capacity I was not sure, because no information was forthcoming. I walked down to the billet, and found the house silent and empty. As I packed my gear, I stood for a few minutes at an upstairs window and watched a Lancaster take-off on air test, in preparation for the night's operations.

It was a nostalgic moment. There was the familiar perimeter track, the curve disappearing into the distance by the dispersal's where the Lancasters stood in unmistakable silhouette, the tiny figures of the ground crews busily ministering to their needs. It was the perimeter I had walked alone so long ago, with my mind in a turmoil of uncertainty; where the skipper had taxied our aircraft around to the runway so often, before the long ordeals to targets like Berlin, Leipzig, Stuttgart, Stettin, and all the other distant objectives that had claimed so many lives.

It had been a period of my life whose influence would

never leave me. As I looked upon all this and remembered, it came to me forcibly: I did not want to leave, I needed the consolation that I was still part of the squadron, of the air crew whose reminiscences I could share. I needed the oily, distinctive smell of that rear turret, the half-fearful anticipation of being called to briefing and, above all, the moments of sheer ecstasy when leaving the enemy coast behind after surviving yet another raid.

What experience in my now certain future was going to compare with all that? It was like being reprieved, set free and hesitating at the gates, bewildered at the normality of everyday life.

Something vital was about to be taken away, but there would be a consolation. It would be apparent when I reached my new posting, for I was to fly with instructor crews, on non-combatant circuits and cross-country exercises, teaching the new crews.

What then? The war, at last, would end: my service would come to a close. Looking back over the long years, I can remember the real anxieties of that moment, when the future changed in prospect from hours to years that stretched on before me into the uncertain, unknown mists of time. In retrospect, that uncertainty remained with me, when I returned to divvy street' like so many others, to marry and bring up two sons, of whom I am proud, and to struggle to earn a decent living without qualifications or trade expertise.

I entered commercial life, which, once the initial impetus of the challenge had worn off, turned into drudgery, that had to be suffered over the years for my family's sake.

The usual mortgage, the thousand and one everyday expenses of respectability, the same bus or train to work, the same newspaper, the sordid fight for promotion, to be able to find a better house, a bigger garden, a more fashionable suburb.

If I sometimes remained on the fringe of the clique in the bar at the local, unwilling to participate in the useless small talk and the limited objectives of those to whom pride in material things reflected clearly how shallow their ambitions and aspirations were, it was because I always felt the urge to get away. Quite often I would. Occasionally my absence would be noticed, resulting in arguments between my wife and myself. Even if transport was readily available, I would walk home, my mind unable to form a conclusive thought. I couldn't find a remedy for this condition despite searching constantly for an answer. How could I when the questions were not fully understood?

This attitude to certain aspects of my life was not one of morbidity nor, I am convinced, of pure cynicism. I did not consider myself superior to people caught in the same rat-race as I was. The solace I found, when I could afford a tiny boat, provided the answer in a number of ways. After spending a weekend on board, I became much more tolerant at work, and in the company of people who would normally have irritated me socially. Each weekday became another step towards the time when I could race off to the moorings some distance away, find some inaccessible cove, anchor off shore and under a night sky, find a peace and understanding solely from the elements themselves. Alternatively, I would be walking in some quiet place where nature forgot its ruthlessness for a while and enthralled me with its beauty.

So life continued. The years flew by, yet only gradually have I overcome my aversion to the insensitive, the unfeeling and, to a lesser extent, to the habitually frivolous, who cannot somehow see the hurt they inflict on others. But I know that my hard-won indifference does nothing to alleviate the suffering they cause to those who cannot, or do not, offer any defence.

How often have I cursed such sensitivity and, in dire moments, criticised myself for my own. Not that I regret my experiences, nor the intensity of my beliefs. An appreciation of the finer things in life is reward enough, a reward which must be earned through experience. If you are deeply sensitive, yet not melancholy, our world is beautiful. Even the ugliness made by man can provide some recompense, for there is beauty everywhere, if you can see it, feel it. Thank providence for the gift of understanding and depth of comprehension.

Now my family are capable of taking care of themselves, aided, I earnestly pray and hope, by any help my wife and I have been able to provide, I long to take to the sea, to cross that horizon for which I have searched so long. Now is the time when my wife and I, with mutual respect, can each amicably leave the other free to realise a cherished ambition, before we find, after the real struggle over the years, that we can only look back at what might have been.

Yet, I am always reminded, and so often comforted, by the profound observation, made by Alan Villiers, one of our more eminent adventurers: 'Anyone of us could have run away before, could have abandoned responsibility to adventure, to the sea, yet it takes more courage to stay behind.'

During the closing months of the war in Europe I endured tedious training flights with a variety of instructor pilots, taking their pupils on cross-country exercises, myself with little to do in the rear turret, except wonder what sort of landings the pupils would make on our return. Some of them were quite spectacular.

I will end my story, with an account of my last operation in a Lancaster. On the 8th May 1945, an announcement was expected hourly of the surrender of the German Forces. Early in the day this took place, VE Day in fact. I put on my best blue in anticipation of the biggest party of all time.

The comments of the aircrew awaiting the opening of the bar when it was announced that we were required in the briefing room, can be imagined. I was listed with a crew made up of senior instructors, all with sixty or seventy ops to their credit, and a pilot of flamboyant character and vast experience, with the rank of Wing Commander.

Our curiosity knew no bounds – what the hell was going on? Churchill was to make the historic announcement on the radio. The war was over, finished, where on earth could we be going and why?

Forty Lancasters from the Group, stripped of all but essentials, were to fly to Lübeck in Northern Germany to airlift Army POWs – thirty-five to each aircraft.

Apart from the satisfaction that the whole operation was so worthwhile, the opportunity to fly unhampered over Europe at peace was indeed a pleasant surprise. A comment from our pilot, 'We'll have a bloody good look around, boys,' as we took off in the morning sunshine, filled me with anticipation. Crossing the North Sea at low level, we overflew three fast-moving torpedo boats coming around in a tight turn, and our exuberant skipper skimmed the wave-tops to shoot up the three boats almost at deck level, with the startled faces of the crews clearly discernible. Our pilot whooped delightedly, remarking: 'That will teach the Navy not to bloody shoot at me again. Do you know, the buggers nearly brought me down over the Thames Estuary in '43.'

That sinister feeling as we crossed the Dutch coast was revived even though the war was over.

'Hope all the Jerries know about the bloody armistice,' a voice remarked, as we skimmed the roof-tops of a large town, where the population were waving excitedly.

Across Germany, we stared aghast at the total destruction in town and city alike. In most cases it was difficult to find a building in any way complete, just skeletons in fields of rubble.

So this was what the thousands of tons of bombs had done, all those awful nights, when I had watched the terrible upheavals below. To see it all in broad daylight from only a few feet above, as the macabre scene unfolded behind me, was like viewing the end of the world.

As we circled the airfield at Lübeck, I could see scores of aircraft parked row upon row below, including a number of

American Flying Fortress bombers. We came in for a perfect landing, and the Wing Commander laughingly remarked: 'Must put on a good show with an audience like this.' After taxying to our position, we were instructed to stay with our aircraft, and on no account to leave the airfield. The ex-prisoners of war were on their way by convoy.

We chatted with other crews, gratefully accepted mugs of tea and sandwiches and, having walked across to talk to the Americans, interestedly looked over their aircraft, which were so completely different from our own. We waited until mid-afternoon, when our irrepressible pilot returned with a large bag, from which he produced two table-lamps and an onyx desk set. 'Souvenirs, old boy,' he said, 'pinched them from the Jerry CO's office.' We were on our way when he called us back: 'Nothing left, you lot, so hang around, they'll be bringing our passengers in a minute.' Grinning triumphantly, he mounted the fuselage ladder to stow his booty.

Then they came, vacating the trucks that queued along the perimeter, men who had endured years of torment in captivity, some since as long ago as Dunkirk, shuffling along with their pitiful, little parcels of meagre belongings, gazing in awe at the might of a hundred four-engined bombers, for them something from another world – a very different world from their distant memories of 1940 when our country had provided such inadequate means against an enemy whose every waking hour had been devoted to the waging of war and to the manufacture of the arms that had produced the blitzkrieg.

The clowning and laughter of the impatient aircrews along the avenues of waiting aircraft ceased abruptly. In the uneasy silence, the shabby groups of POWs were allocated – thirty-five to each Lancaster, twenty or so to the Americans. Our groups sat on the grass in the warm sunshine, with two of them, ill and emaciated, lying on stretchers.

I passed among them, handing out large, waxed paper bags in case they should become air-sick on the flight home.

All my efforts to encourage conversation were of no avail: they responded neither to us nor to each other, following any instruction with a numb obedience. I wanted to say to each one, 'It's all right now, I can only try and understand what you have been through, but we are proud to be here to take you home.' Instead, it was only by smile and gesture that I could endeavour to show my feelings.

It fell to me to seat them all as comfortably as possible, along each side of the sparse interior of the fuselage. This was devoid of any proper seating, but a distribution of blankets helped and, at last, the crew took their places for take-off.

As I eased myself into the rear turret, I turned and gave them a thumbs-up sign, receiving a faint smile from several anxious faces, while the others sat unheeding as the roar of the engines reached a crescendo. The waiting was long and interminable, the queue of aircraft never ending, edging its way to the runway.

Anxious about our passengers' welfare, I opened the turret and bulkhead doors to look back along the interior of the aircraft. I was hoping that the warm atmosphere, and the smell of oil and dope that always lingered there, had not caused any discomfort. Most of them looked blankly back at me, but, by miming the wiping of sweat from my brow and indicating the flow of cool air from the open doors, I managed to gain some response from our charges. The thumbs-up signal again, and I locked myself in as, at last, we turned for take-off.

This our skipper accomplished with practised ease, flying at low level across the German countryside, which looked not unlike our own. It was all over for the people down there, too. I mused upon their feelings as they saw the fleet of aircraft, which they must have heard so often high in the darkened heavens, now speeding low over their homes.

Over the sea, sparkling in the early evening sun, the skipper gave me the clearance to leave the turret and, after checking to ensure the lock was engaged, I eased along backwards until I could join our passengers. I sympathised with those who had been air-sick, and handed out more paper bags. One or two of the more adventurous were persuaded to climb into the mid-upper turret, and it was with some difficulty that each in turn was induced to come down and give his friends the opportunity to enjoy the novelty. Our pilot even allowed visits up front, and I had a busy time conducting our now eager passengers back and forth past the cramped positions of the wireless operator and the navigator.

As the English coast appeared below, a corporal, whom I had just positioned up forward, leaned over eagerly, his face aglow with excitement. It was all too much: at the sight of his beloved homeland tears ran down his cheeks. I put my arm around his shoulders as he sobbed. After we had landed, at an airfield where the hangars had been converted into a reception area, I opened the door and lowered the ladder into place. A large crowd of cheering WAAFs and nurses were waiting. I gave a mock bow, perfectly well aware who they were anxious to greet. The soldiers climbed down, bewildered, to be ushered across the tarmac with an attentive female on each arm. An ambulance took away the two stretcher-cases.

I watched the others go until they had passed through into the reception centre, while another Lancaster slowly approached to unload. I pulled up the boarding ladder and slammed the door hard and engaged the lock. The sound echoed hollowly in the empty cavern of the fuselage. After signalling to the wireless operator forward that all was OK, I slithered down to the turret, and the Lancaster moved off. A green to go and, without stopping, the skipper gave full power as the aircraft lined up after turning off the perimeter. The runway receded as we gained height, and I could see the lights from the reception centre flooding the forecourt. A crowd of tiny figures were looking up.

It had been a good day. I plugged into the heating circuit, and lit a cigarette. The airfield lights faded into the distance.

Victory Message

To: The Path Finder Force.
From: Air Vice-Marshal D. C. T. Bennett, CB, CBE, DSO

Great Britain and the Commonwealth have made a contribution to the civilised world so magnificent that history alone will be able to appreciate it fully. Through disaster and triumph, sometimes supported and sometimes alone, the British races have steadfastly and energetically over many long years flung their forces against the international criminals. They have fought the war from end to end without a moment's respite, in all theatres, and with all arms – land, sea and air.

Bomber Command's share in this great effort has been a major one. You, each one of you, have made that possible. The Path Finder Force has shouldered a grave responsibility. It has led Bomber Command, the greatest striking force ever known. That we have been successful can be seen in the far-reaching results which the Bomber offensive has achieved. That is the greatest reward the Path Finder Force ever hopes to receive, for those results have benefited all law-abiding peoples.

Whilst you have been hard at work through these vital years, I have not interrupted you, as I would like to have done, with messages of praise and congratulation. You were too busy; but now that your great contribution to the world has been made, I want to thank you each man and woman of you personally and to congratulate you on your unrelenting spirit and energy and on the results you have achieved.

Happiness to you all – always. Keep Pressing On along the Path of Peace.

DON BENNETT.

Headquarters, Path Finder Force,
European V-Day, 1945.

BOMBER COMMAND

Monthly Table of Sorties Dispatched and Aircraft Missing or Crashed

		Sorties		Missing		Crashed		Percentage Missing and Crashed	
		NIGHT	DAY	NIGHT	DAY	NIGHT	DAY	NIGHT	DAY
1939	September	83	40	2	12	3	0	6.0	30.0
	October	32	0	2	0	2	0	12.5	–
	November	15	4	0	0	1	0	–	–
	December	40	119	0	17	0	2	–	16.0
1940	January	38	6	0	0	0	0	–	–
	February	54	4	1	0	2	0	5.8	–
	March	239	53	5	1	6	0	4.6	1.9
	April	489	167	18	15	8	0	5.3	9.0
	May	1,617	802	21	49	3	3	1.5	6.5
	June	2,484	812	26	31	7	1	1.3	3.9
	July	1,722	616	40	32	3	4	2.5	5.8
	August	2,188	417	52	18	11	0	2.9	4.3
	September	3,141	98	65	1	21	0	2.7	1.0
	October	2,242	172	27	1	32	0	2.6	0.6
	November	1,894	113	50	2	34	0	4.4	1.8
	December	1,385	56	37	2	25	0	4.2	3.6
1941	January	1,030	96	12	3	12	1	2.3	4.2
	February	1,617	124	16	2	32	2	3.0	3.2
	March	1,728	162	35	4	36	0	4.1	2.5
	April	2,249	676	56	23	12	7	3.0	4.4

May	2,416	273	39	20	14	3	2.2	8.4
June	3,228	531	76	22	15	3	2.8	4.7
July	3,243	582	91	55	28	3	3.7	11.8
August	3,354	468	121	35	45	5	5.0	8.5
September	2,621	263	76	14	62	1	5.3	5.7
October	2,501	138	68	17	40	1	4.3	13.0
November	1,713	43	83	0	21	0	6.0	–
December	1,411	151	36	7	16	0	3.1	4.6
1942 January	2,216	24	56	0	32	1	4.0	–
February	1,162	252	18	15	14	0	2.7	6.3
March	2,224	131	78	2	21	2	4.4	1.5
April	3,752	246	130	13	29	0	4.2	6.1
May	2,702	105	114	1	21	1	5.0	0.9
June	4,801	196	199	2	39	1	5.0	1.5
July	3,914	313	171	19	22	0	4.9	6.1
August	2,454	186	142	10	16	5	6.4	8.1
September	3,489	127	169	6	39	0	6.0	4.7
October	2,193	106	89	14	27	0	5.8	3.4
November	2,067	127	53	11	23	0	3.7	8.6
December	1,758	200	72	16	22	2	5.3	9.0
1943 January	2,556	406	86	15	18	3	4.1	4.4
February	5,030	426	101	6	22	3	2.4	2.1
March	5,174	284	161	7	25	1	3.6	2.8
April	5,571	316	253	12	24	1	5.0	4.1
May	5,130	360	234	19	27	4	5.1	6.4
June	5,816	0	275	0	15	0	5.0	–

	Month								
	July	6,170	0	188	0	31	0	3.5	–
	August	7,807	0	275	0	33	0	3.9	–
	September	5,513	0	191	0	34	0	4 1	–
	October	4	638	0	159	0	21	0	3.9
	November	5,208	0	152	0	48	0	4.0	–
	December	4,123	0	170	0	47	0	5.3	–
1944	January	6,278	0	314	0	38	0	5.6	–
	February	4,263	45	199	0	21	0	5.2	–
	March	9,031	18	283	0	39	0	3.6	–
	April	9,873	10	214	0	25	0	2.4	–
	May	11,353	16	274	0	29	0	2.7	–
	June	13,592	2,371	293	12	30	0	2.4	0.5
	July	11,500	6,293	229	12	29	4	2.2	0.3
	August	10,013	10,271	186	36	22	1	2.1	0.3
	September	6,428	9,643	96	41	15	0	1.8	0.4
	October	10,193	6,713	75	52	26	0	1.0	0.8
	November	9,589	5,055	98	41	34	0	1.4	0.8
	December	11,239	3,656	88	31	43	0	1.2	0.8
1945	January	9,603	1,304	121	12	57	0	1.9	0.6
	February	13,715	3,685	164	9	60	0	1.6	0.2
	March	11,585	9,606	168	47	76	10	2.1	0.6
	April	8,822	5,001	51	22	25	6	0.9	0.5
	May	360	1,863	3	0	0	1	0.9	0.6

1939–45 (Those shown as crashed were damaged so badly by fighters, flak or other causes that they were written of 11.

BOMBER COMMAND AIRCREW KILLED 1939–1945

COUNTRY	POPULATION (1940)	CASUALTIES	PERCENTAGE OF TOTAL CASUALTIES	CASUALTIES AS A PERCENTAGE OF POPULATION
Britain	46,889,000	38,462 – RAF	69.2	0.082
Canada	11,506,655	9,919 – RCAF	17.8	0.085
Australia	6,929,691	4,050 – RAAF	7.3	0.059
New Zealand	1,491,484	1,679 – RNZAF	3.0	0.113
Poland	35,000,000	929 – Polish	1.7	–
		500 – Other	1.0	
		55,539 – Total	100.0	

REAR GUNNER

I feared for him.
His mind.
What he saw
hurtling backwards
to his private war.

He could spare only
a fleeting thought
for the enemy, in the city,
staring up, or hiding from the sound,
of a thousand Merlins
circling around.

When he glanced down
into the target's molten lead
incinerating the living,
or dead!
Suspended four miles high,
in fear and cold,
it was retaliation
he'd been told.

What words descriptive enough to tell,
of a comradeship in hell.
Or explain
what the torment was like
to have to come again, again.
Eight hours or more
is an age – on age!
With only a perspex capsule
for a stage.

As his friends,
torn asunder in the tortured air
to know only roundabout
the dank, grey clouds,
as shrouds!

On return to base
he couldn't grieve;

or a quiet moment spend,
or really quite believe
the absence of a particular friend.

From another crew
who only yesterday he knew.
In any case, it wasn't done.

There are no sops' tonight
an evening out instead
maybe only a twenty-four hour future
lies ahead.
Drink too many beers! Dance!
Find a girl! Laugh! Sing! -anything.
To hide that inner mind
already dead.

At times his face
told of a recent leave
normality to retrace.
Not this hideous make believe,
this stark, unreal contrast to home
where there was 'sameness'
nothing re-arranged.
In the sudden quietness of his room
staring, dreadful at the papered wall
in his own bed curled
sheltered briefly from that other world
trying the everyday things to recall.

Down the lane,
the old stone school.
Village tea shops, bright awnings
steadfast chapel, Boys' Brigade,
and breakfast on slow Sunday mornings.

The war took its course
he older, but young in years
still has no tears.
I feared for him more then
for what he saw, now lies

deep, unanswered in his eyes.
   Some evenings in
the village inn at times, he hears the idle talk begin
and at the outside of the crowd
he quietly leaves
and has to be alone.
Hardly speaking, yet not proud
not feeling better than they
because he had hardly anything to say.
As he walks, his mind still wanders,
and in so many different ways
living in the memory
of their living days.
   RON SMITH DFM

NO. 156 (PATHFINDER) SQUADRON

Formed at Thetford, Norfolk on 12th October 1918 with the intention of being equipped with DH9a's. No aircraft were received before the Squadron was disbanded at the end of November 1918.

The Squadron was re-formed on 14th February 1942 at Alconbury, Huntingdonshire as a medium-bomber squadron equipped with Wellingtons. Initially the Squadron operated with 3 Group, Bomber Command but in August 1942 was selected as one of four Squadrons to form the nucleus of Air Vice-Marshal D. C. T. Bennett's elite Pathfinder Force of 8 Group. (Squadron motto: 'We light the Way'.)

In early 1943 the Squadron converted from Wellingtons to Lancasters and operated from Pathfinder Force bases at RAF Warboys and RAF Upwood in Huntingdonshire. In April 1943 the Australian government decided to raise money for the war effort through a series of war loan tours with a distinguished all-Australian crew flying the first Lancaster to Australia via Canada, the USA, Hawaii and Fiji. 156 Squadron had the honour of supplying the crew (captain F/Lt Peter Isaacson) and the Lancaster was given a tumultuous welcome when it arrived at Amberley, Queensland on 3rd June 1943.

156 Squadron played an immensely important role in Bomber Command's offensive against major German targets-marking targets with incendiaries and flares and during its thirty-eight months of operations dropping over 16,000 tons of bombs on the enemy. During Ron Smith's period with the Squadron (late 1943 -mid 1944) many crews became well-known under the captaincy of their respective pilots-Jack Cuthill, 'Ginger' Cleland, 'Kiwi' Cockrane, 'Drunky' Owen, 'Paul' Temple, 'Dinghy' Etchells, etc. and were decorated as the number of sorties grew-the 'Big City'

several times, operations into the Ruhr Valley, the notorious Nuremberg raid, targets farther afield such as Stettin, Stuttgart, Augsburg, daylight raids on marshalling yards and V-weapon sites in France and Belgium as well as mine-laying operations.

On 1st April 1944 nearly all 'B' Flight and its aircraft, together with a Flight from 7 Squadron, Pathfinder Force, moved to Little Staughton, in Bedfordshire, to form 582 Squadron.

156 Squadron was disbanded in September 1945. Its losses on operations totalled 45 Wellingtons and 117 Lancasters.

The Squadron's honours list included 22 DSOs, I bar to the DSO, 296 DFCs, 22 bars to DFCs, 5 CGMs (Flying), 110 DFMs, I bar to the DFM, and I BEM.

Squadron Commanders

W/Cdr R. N. Cook	30.7.42–28.10.42
W/Cdr T. S. Rivett-Carnac DFC	28.10.42–8.6.43
G/Capt R. W. P. Collings AFC	8.6.43–15.1.44
W/Cdr E. C. Eaton DFC	15.1.44–27.4.44
W/Cdr T. L. Bingham-Hall DFC (later G/Capt DSO, DFC)	27.4.44–21.11.44
W/Cdr D. B. Falconer DFC, AFC	21.11.44–30.12.44
W/Cdr T. E. Ison DSO, DFC	30.12.44–10.4.45
W/Cdr A. J. L. Craig, DSO, DFC	10.4.45–disbandment

Other Goodall paperbacks from Crécy Publishing Ltd

Lancaster To Berlin

F/Lt Walter Thompson DFC & Bar
As a Pathfinder Walter Thompson led
the bombing raids into Germany.
Above all, he flew to Berlin, in the
thick of the 1943-44 offensive against
'The Big City'.
200 pages, paperback B format
illustrated.
ISBN 0907579 37 X. £4.99

Air Gunner

Mike Henry
The experiences of an air gunner flying
in the Blenheims of RAF 2 Group,
who was lucky enough to survive a
conflict in which so many young air
gunners perished.
200 pages, paperback B format
illustrated.
ISBN 0907579 42 6. £4.99

Uncommon Valour

A.G. Goulding DFM
A comprehensive view of Bomber
Command's part in the Second World
War and an important re-appraisal of
the importance of Bomber Command
in World War Two.
192 pages, paperback B format
illustrated,
ISBN 0 85979 095 9. £4.99

Wing Leader

Air Vice-Marshal 'Johnnie' Johnson
The thrilling story of the top-scoring
Allied fighter pilot of World War Two.
320 pages, paperback B format.
ISBN 0 85979 090 8. £4.99

Night Flyer

S/Ldr Lewis Brandon DSO DFC &
Bar
The exciting story of one of the most
successful RAF night fighting
partnerships of WW2.
208 pages, paperback.
ISBN 0 907579 16 7. £3.99

Enemy Coast Ahead

W/Cdr Guy Gibson VC DSO & Bar
DFC & Bar
The autobiography of Guy Gibson VC,
one of the greatest books written about
RAF Bomber Command in WW2.
288 pages, paperback.
ISBN 0 907579 08 6. £3.99

No Moon Tonight

Don Charlwood
A Bomber Command classic, a book of
deep feelings depicting the human cost
of the Bomber Command air war.
192 pages, paperback.
ISBN 0 907579 06 X. £3.99

A WAAF in Bomber Command

"Pip" Beck
The story of an R/T operator in
Bomber Command who talked down
bomber crews returning from
operations, met them off-duty and, all
too often, mourned their loss.
171 pages, paperback.
ISBN 0 907579 12 4. £3.99

Beyond The Dams To The Tirpitz

Alan Cooper
The is story of 617 squadron – The
Dambusters – and their 95 further
operations after the famous dambuster
raid, including their part in the
destruction of the *Tirpitz*.
198 pages, paperback.
ISBN 0 907579 15 9. £3.99

Wings Over Georgia

S/Ldr Jack Currie DFC
The story of Jack Currie's entry into
the RAF, his early training in the UK,
initial flying training with the US
Army Air Corps and return to England
to join Bomber Command.
154 pages, paperback.
ISBN 0 907579 11 6 £3.99

Lancaster Target

S/Ldr Jack Currie DFC
Described as one of the best three
books about life in Bomber Command,
Lancaster Target is the story of one
crew's fight to fly and survive a full
tour of operations in the night skies of
wartime Europe. *Lancaster Target*
featured in the award-winning BBC
documentary 'The Lancaster Legend'.
200 pages, paperback B format
illustrated.
ISBN 0907579 32 9. £4.99

Mosquito Victory

S/Ldr Jack Currie DFC
The compelling, highly readable sequel
to *Lancaster Target*, graphically
describing the life of an RAF bomber
pilot on 'rest', first instructing trainees
on the four-engined Halifax bomber,
then flying gliders, and lastly posted to
the élite Pathfinder force.
176 pages, paperback B format. ISBN
0 85979 091 6. £3.99

Evader

Denys Teare

A story of escape and evasion behind enemy lines

On September 5th 1943, Teare baled out of his burning Lancaster bomber over Occupied France; from this moment on he was an evader in the midst of the enemy. Teare became a doubly wanted man: not only a British airman evading the occupying force, but also an active member of the French Resistance.

256 pages hardback with photographs throughout.

ISBN 0 85979 096 7. £16.95

Sigh For A Merlin

Alex Henshaw

A truly classic book. In September 1940, when production of the Supermarine Spitfire was moved to Castle Bromwich near Birmingham, Alex Henshaw was appointed Chief Test Pilot. Here he test flew production Spitfires – it is now estimated that he personally flew over 10% of all the Spitfires ever built. He also flew another Merlin-engined classic – the Lancaster.

256 pages hardback with photographs throughout.

ISBN 0 85979 092 4. £19.95

Spitfire, A Test Pilot's Story

Jeffrey Quill OBE

The personal account of an exceptional test pilot. Jeffrey Quill describes the early problems of mass production of the Spitfire, of developing its capabilities, of dealing with its defects, and of the qualities which made the Spitfire a truly great aeroplane.

320 pages hardback with photographs throughout.

ISBN 0 85979 093 2. £19.95

We Landed By Moonlight

Group Captain Hugh Verity DSO* DFC

The secret RAF landings in France 1940 - 1944

The only comprehensive record of the clandestine operations of the special duties squadrons, supported the French resistance and Special Operations Executive (SOE) – landing in unprepared fields to deposit and collect agents, downed airmen and other human cargo; and returning to base, still avoiding detection.

254 pages hardback with photographs throughout.

ISBN 0 85979 114 9. £16.95

Nine Lives

Air Commodore Alan Deere DSO, CBE, DFC and bar

This famous New Zealand fighter pilot describes his RAF career from Munich Crisis, the Battle of Britain (during which he had to 'bale-out' no less than three times) and up to the D-Day operations.

262 pages hardback with photographs throughout.

ISBN 1 873454 01 5. £14.95

Battle Under The Moon

S/Ldr Jack Currie DFC

The RAF raid on Mailly-le-Camp, 1944

Battle Under The Moon chronicles the ill-fated RAF raid on the Panzer tank depot and military barracks at Mailly-le-Camp in preparation for the D-Day landings. It is a spellbinding account of that night and the aftermath, including the story of those who were shot down and evaded capture with the help of the French resistance.

192 pages hardback with photographs throughout.

ISBN 0 85979 109 2. £14.95

I Learned About Flying from That

Various authors
Pilots confess some of the worst moments of their flying careers, from the column of the same name in Pilot magazine.
196 pages hardback with photographs throughout.
ISBN 1 874783 45 4. £12.95

2 Group RAF

Michael J F Bower
A complete history 1936-1945
The history of 2 group, from costly daylight operations in the Norwegian and French campaigns, to Malta and intruder raids into Germany.
532 pages with photographs.
ISBN 0947554203. £23.95

Fighter Squadrons Of The RAF

John D R Rawlings
and their aircraft
A unique reference work – the histories of the 241 squadrons of RAF Fighter Command, with 23 appendices.
600 pages with photographs.
ISBN 0947554246 £29.95

Pathfinder Force

Gordon Musgrove
A history of 8 group RAF
The record of how AVM Bennett built up the Pathfinders, pinpointing and marking targets for the main force bombers.
302 pages with photographs.
ISBN 0947554238 £15.95

Twenty-One Squadrons

Leslie Hunt
The history of the Royal Auxiliary Air Force 1925-1957
The full story of the famous 'weekend' squadrons, who served fro Europe to Burma
432 pages with photographs.
ISBN 0947554262 £23.95

The First Pathfinders

Ken Wakefield
The operational history of Kampfgruppe 100, 1939-1941
After the failure of daylight bombing raids, the Luftwaffe perfected a technique for pinpointing and marking bomber targets at night – Pathfinding.
250 pages with photographs.
ISBN 0947554203 £15.95

The History Of The German Night Fighter Force

Gebhard Aders
1917 - 1945
A rare insight into the Luftwaffe's night fighter force – the men, machines and equipment.
284 pages with photographs.
ISBN 0947554217 £15.95

The Story Of 609 Squadron

Frank Ziegler
Under the white rose
The multi-national Auxiliary squadron who flew Spitfires in the Battle of Britain, and later Typhoons into Europe.
476 pages with photographs.
ISBN 0947554297 £16.95

Crécy Hardback Books

Heavenly Days
James Pelly-Fry DSO
Recollections of a contented airman
Autobiography of the man who
became PA to Arthur Harris, led the
Bostons of 88 squadron and became
equerry to King George VI.
400 pages with photographs.
ISBN 0947554327 £18.95

Clean Sweep
Tony Spooner DSO DFC
The life of Air Marshal Sir Ivor Broom
KCB, CBE, DFC + 2 bars, AFC
The remarkable story of a lad from the
Rhondda Valley who rose from
Sergeant pilot to Air Marshal.
244 pages with photographs.
ISBN 0947554505 £17.99

Fighter Pilot; George Barclay
edited by Humphrey Wynn
A self portrait
The outstanding story of the Battle of
Britain pilot, later shot down over
France but escaped back to England,
only to be shot down and killed in
North Africa in 1942.
224 pages with photographs.
ISBN 0947554475 £16.99

Valiant Wings
Norman Franks
Battle and Blenheim squadrons over
France 1940
The ten Battle squadrons and four
Blenheim squadrons which supported
the BEF in the Battle of France, and
later in the Dunkirk evacuation.
298 pages with photographs.
ISBN 0947554491 £17.99

Brothers In Arms
Chris Goss
The story of a British & German
fighter unit during the Battle of Britain
A view from both sides of the conflict
– 609 Squadron flying Spitfires,
1/JG53 flying Me109Es, from August
to October 1940.
200 pages with photographs.
ISBN 0947554378 £19.99

Warburton's War
Tony Spooner
The life of W/C Adrain Warburton
DSO, DFC (US)
A lively account of the 'misfit' pilot,
who became one of the RAF's most
decorated pilots before he was
mysteriously lost flying a P-38
Lightning near the end of the war.
240 pages with photographs. ISBN
0947554467 £16.99

Duel Under The Stars
Wilhelm Johnen
A German night fighter pilot during
WWII
The author was a high scoring Knight's
Cross holder, who also writes about
NJG1 personalities such as Lent,
Schnaufer and Wittgenstein.
240 pages with photographs.
ISBN 0947554424 £16.99

Shark Squadron
Robin Brown

The history of 112 squadron 1917 -
1975
The complete history, from Sopwith
Camels in WWI, through desert
warfare in WWII, to post-war Hunters,
still with the famous 'shark's mouth'
markings.
300 pages with photographs.
ISBN 0947554335 £24.99

It's Suicide But It's Fun

Chris Goss
The story of 102 squadron
From its aircrew and the opposing
forces a chronicle of 102 squadron
who, flying Halifaxes in WWII,
suffered the third highest casualty rate
in Bomber Command.
224 pages with photographs.
ISBN 0947554599 £19.99

Mosquito

C Martin Sharpe & Michael J F
Bowyer
The definite history of the de Havilland
Mosquito, fully revised and up-dated
with many new photographs.
540 pages with photographs.
ISBN 0947554416 £29.99

The Blue Arena

Bob Spurdle
The New Zealander Battle of Britain
ace who went on to fly against the
Japanese before being grounded after
an extraordinary 564 sorties
264 pages with photographs.
ISBN 0947554580 £17.50

Reap The Whirlwind

Spencer Dunmore & William Carter
The untold story of 6 Group RAF,
Canada's bomber force
The Canadian Bomber Force was
formed within the RAF in 1942, they
played a vital part in the bomber battle,
flying Lancasters and Halifaxes.
464 pages with photographs.
ISBN 0947554357 £19.95

Wellington Wings

F R Chappell
An RAF intelligence officer in the
Western desert
Based on diaries kept from 1942-1945,
a vivid picture of life and death in a
desert bomber group.
282 pages with photographs.
ISBN 0947554270 £15.95

Paddy Finucane

Doug Stokes Fighter Ace
Irishman Brendan 'Paddy' Finucane
was a true fighter ace, with 32 victories
at the time of his death in 1942.
220 pages with photographs.
ISBN 094755422X £14.95

Ace Of Aces; M T StJ Pattle

E C R Baker
With the greatest number of confirmed
'kills' in WW2, South African 'Pat'
Pattle is recognised as the top-scoring
Allied fighter pilot.
248 pages with photographs.
ISBN 094755436X £15.95

Wings Of The Night

Alexander Hamilton
The secret missions of Grp Capt
Pickard DSO, DFC
An outstanding pilot, flying agents in
and out of enemy territory, Pickard was
killed leading the daylight Mosquito
raid on Amiens prison to release
French Resistance leaders.
208 pages with photographs.
ISBN 0947554343 £14.95

Low Attack

John Woolridge
The story of two Mosquito squadrons
1940-1943
The author was commander of 105
squadron, when it made the celebrated
attacks on the Gestapo HQ in Oslo, the
engine works in Copenhagen and the
first daylight raid on Berlin.
176 pages with photographs. ISBN
0947554319 £14.95

Sky Tiger

Norman Franks
The story of 'Sailor' Malan
Britain's premier fighter pilot who shot
down 35 enemy aircraft, a record that
remained in Europe for three years
222 pages with photographs.
ISBN 0947554386 £16.99

The Enemy Is Listening

Aileen Clayton
The story of the Y service
The author was an intelligence officer
in the Y service – the radio listening
branch of the RAF.
382 pages with photographs.
ISBN 0947554289 £17.50

Jack's War

C G Connell
Lower-Deck recollections from WWII
A book about ordinary seamen and life
aboard and in action on every type of
ship in the Royal Navy
263 pages with photographs.
ISBN 0947554556 £17.50

Eagle's War

Peter C Smith
The war story of HMS *Eagle*
The carrier HMS Eagle saw action first
in the Indian Ocean, then in the
Mediterranean. It provided Malta's
only aerial defence in the Battle of
Calabria, but was finally sunk by
German torpedoes in 1942.
224 pages with photographs.
ISBN 0947554602 £18.99

Operations Most Secret

Ian Trenowden
SOE - the Malayan theatre
A rare account of Special Operations
executive operations in Malaya and the
Far East which put a total of 400 men
into Japanese occupied territory
232 pages with photographs.
ISBN 0947554432 £16.99

Fighting Destroyer

C G Connell
The story of HMS *Petard*
The story of the ship that sank three
enemy submarines – one German, one
Italian and one Japanese.
272 pages with photographs. ISBN
0947554408 £16.99

Pedestal

Peter C Smith
The Malta Convoy of August 1942
The story of the battle to reach the
embattled island of Malta, still
resisting the Axis forces but in danger
of being starved of supplies.
256 pages with photographs.
ISBN 0947554483 £16.99

The Hunting Submarine

Ian Trenowden
The fighting life of HMS *Tally-Ho*
The spectacular success of HMS *Tally-Ho*, a T-class submarine which took a heavy toll on enemy shipping.
224 pages with photographs.
ISBN 0947554394 £16.99

Arctic Victory

Peter C Smith
The story of convoy PQ18
In 1942 the climax of the war at sea was reached with three tremendous convoy battles, one in the Mediterranean and two in the Arctic. After the annihilation of PQ17, all rested on PQ18.
240 pages with photographs.
ISBN 0947554440 £16.99

Operation Bolero
Ken Wakefield

The Americans in Bristol and the West Country 1942-45

The build-up of American forces in the West Country in preparation for the D-Day landings; the 9th Air Force and the 12th Army Group including the 1st Army, 3rd Army and 9th Army.
144 pages with photographs.
ISBN 0947554513 £12.50

Task Force 57

Peter C Smith
The British Pacific fleet 1944-1945
The story of the largest British fleet of WWII. Formed to fight Germany, it was instead sent to Japan, fighting alongside the American fleets
206 pages with photographs.
ISBN 0947554459 £16.99

Sakishima

Stuart Eadon
and back
The author served aboard HMS *Berwick* on Russian convoy, the carrier HMS *Formidable* in the Mediterranean and finally HMS *Indefatigable* in the Pacific.
312 pages with photographs.
ISBN 0947554564 £17.99

Kamikaze

Stuart Eadon
The story of the British Pacific fleet
The tremendous history of the British Pacific Fleet 1944-1945, as told by over 200 men from 60 ships.
832 pages with photographs.
ISBN 0947554610 £24.99

Steathily By Night

Ian Trenowden
Clandestine beach operations in WWII
The history of the Combined Operations Pilotage Parties, put ashore to survey land and coastline behind enemy lines to prepare for invasion.
272 pages with photographs. ISBN 0947554548 £18.99

Crécy Publishing Ltd, Southside, Manchester Airport, Wilmslow, Cheshire SK9 4LL
UK. Tel: 0161 499 0024
Fax: 0161 499 0298
email: books@airplan.u-net.com
CompuServe 101727.3000